Student Study Guide with Map Exercises

for use with

Nation of Nations
A Concise Narrative of the American Republic

Third Edition

Volume One

James West Davidson

William E. Gienapp
Harvard University

Christine Leigh Heyrman
University of Delaware

Mark Lytle
Bard College

Michael B. Stoff
University of Texas--Austin

Prepared by
Linda Killen
Radford University

Boston   Burr Ridge, IL   Dubuque, IA   Madison, WI   New York   San Francisco   St. Louis
Bangkok   Bogotá   Caracas   Kuala Lumpur   Lisbon   London   Madrid   Mexico City
Milan   Montreal   New Delhi   Santiago   Seoul   Singapore   Sydney   Taipei   Toronto

McGraw-Hill Higher Education

A Division of The **McGraw-Hill** *Companies*

Student Study Guide with Map Exercises for use with
Nation of Nations: A Concise Narrative of the American Republic
Davidson/Gienapp/Heyrman/Lytle/Stoff/Killen

1 2 3 4 5 6 7 8 9 0 BKM/BKM 0 9 8 7 6 5 4 3 2 1

ISBN 0-07-241960-1

www.mhhe.com

CONTENTS

INTRODUCTION

This Study Guide is designed to accompany *Nation of Nations: A Concise Narrative of the American Republic*. In it, we try to help you organize more clearly the facts and themes presented in the text and to present that material more cogently in exams and papers. Ultimately, we hope, the guide may even help you to come to grips with the history of a nation that has shaped us all in countless ways. To quote from the preface of the text itself, "History supplies our very identity—a sense of the social groups to which we belong, whether family, ethnic group, race, class, or gender. It reveals to us the foundations of our deepest religious beliefs and traces the roots of our economic and political systems. It explores how we celebrate or grieve, sing the songs we sing, weather the illnesses to which time and chance subject us. It commands our attention for these good reasons and for no good reason at all, other than a fascination with the way the myriad tales play out."

A Critical Approach to Reading History

In the days before the consumer movement dictated that warnings be affixed to hazardous products, the traditional attitude of most sellers was summed up in the Latin motto, *caveat emptor*: Let the buyer beware. We have not affixed warning labels to our text, but we would like to make it clear that buyers should be more than a little wary when reading any history—including our own.

Why? All history is presented in a way that is slightly seductive. Textbooks come dressed out in the full trappings of authority. They present the printed word on crisp white pages, provide a host of detailed maps, charts, and appendices, plus a list of authors with university affiliations after their names. The subliminal message behind all these trappings is: *This book is authoritative. This is history the way it* really *happened. Read and believe.* When, of course, the truth is much more complicated.

Look, for example, at the following paragraph, taken from Chapter 2 of *Nation of Nations*.

> *Even the most skeptical immigrants must have been shocked at what they found. The death rate in Virginia in the 1620s was higher than in England during times of epidemic disease. The life expectancy for Chesapeake men who reached the age of 20 was a mere 48 years; for women it was lower still. Servants fared worst of all, since malnutrition, overwork, and abuse made them vulnerable to disease. As masters scrambled to make quick profits, they extracted the maximum amount of work before death carried off their laborers. An estimated 40 percent of servants never regained their freedom because they did not survive to the end of their indentured terms.*

On the face of it, the paragraph seems straightforward. It is not an impassioned argument filled with value judgments about whether Christopher Columbus was a hero or a villain or whether the Civil War could have been avoided. It merely describes the harsh conditions of life in early Virginia.

But the word *merely* is misleading. This paragraph lists a number of statistics as if they were obvious, easily documented truths. For example it says that male Virginians who reached the age of 20 had, on average, a life expectancy of only 48. None of these "facts" are recorded in some official *Virginia Book of Records*, like Guinness's famous collection. And none of the authors of this text have themselves combed through the old documents, records of births and deaths, records of the plague in England, to make these computations. We have relied on other historians who have done this work and published it, just as they rely on our work in other specialized areas. Often, years of research lie behind such apparently simple statements. The computations are often difficult and full of uncertainty. Yet readers of a text like this will quickly read and digest those few sentences and quickly move on to another paragraph—equally full of uncertainties. *Read and believe.*

There is no way, of course, for readers to skeptically check the research behind hundreds of different subjects and thousands of paragraphs in any history text. Yet it is worth understanding, right at the start, that a text is inevitably misleading in its presentation. To compress an account of American history even into an ample 1,000 pages means leaving out most of the uncertainties behind any statement of "facts."

Beyond that, larger uncertainties await in matters of interpretation. The authors have had to make hard choices about presenting and interpreting American history. These decisions must be made chapter by chapter, and even sentence by sentence. How much biographical information should one include of pivotal figures like Washington, Lincoln, or King? How much on the history of anonymous Americans like shoemakers in nineteenth-century Massachusetts? Such decisions are not merely questions of space. They involve larger issues of interpretation. Do individual actions shape history more than broad social forces and trends? Is it more important to talk about the rise of a market economy or the rise of the modern presidency? Putting words to paper involves making choices about a host of different issues, both large and small.

In the limited space available to a textbook, it is impossible to explore in any detail so many differences of interpretation. But, as alert readers, you should be aware that those differences remain, always lurking below the narrative's confident surface. One goal of this Study Guide is to help students become more sensitive to the choices historians must inevitably make.

How to Use This Study Guide

The guide provides a **Keys to the Chapter** section to help you identify the main ideas and pieces of knowledge you should take from the chapter. It also contains both **Review Questions** that are designed to help you review for exams, as well as a **Critical Thinking** section designed to hone skills that are crucial for analyzing historical problems and writing concise, coherent essays, research papers and examinations. The material is presented as follows:

Learning Objectives. These list the chapter's five or six most important themes. They serve as a means of reviewing key material that is likely to be covered on exams. In fact, they could be treated as exam questions: If you find you can't answer each of them coherently, you need additional preparation.

The Chapter in Perspective places the chapter under review within the larger context of American history. It provides links to materials discussed in previous chapters and/or identifies trends that will become important in future chapters.

Overview. This provides a summary of the chapter's major themes, using the same headings that appear in the chapter itself. You may wish to read the Overview before beginning your reading, as a preview of the material. Or read afterward, the Overview serves as a tool for review. Summaries like these do not include all the facts and interpretive material that you will need to discuss key themes and topics. They do focus attention on those areas you would naturally elaborate upon in an exam.

Key Events are timeline chronologies. Use them as a checklist of important occurrences and trends, but also consider how they relate to each other in sequence in order to develop a sense of the pacing of history. How long were the Pilgrims in Massachusetts before John Winthrop's Puritans arrived? (Chapter 3) Timelines allow you to better sense the progression of events and the matter of historical timing.

Multiple-Choice Questions. Although the questions cover a representative range of topics, they are not meant to be exhaustive—only to provide a general feel for the *type* of factual questions that may be asked on an exam. Following each item is a page reference, indicating where the answer may be found.

Completion. These paragraph-style exercises allow you to test your knowledge in a contextualized fashion. Use them as a final review of your comprehension of the material covered in the chapter.

Identifications. These include terms, concepts, individuals, and places. If you can explain the significance of all of them, you should be well prepared to handle the factual aspects of the chapter material.

Map Exercises. Many chapters include an outline map, where you are asked to locate significant places or other geographic information central to the period.

Essay Questions. These cover a range of topics of the sort that might be on any exam. In using the questions for review, it may not be necessary to write out an entire sample essay, although putting something to paper is always a superior way to organize your thoughts. (It is remarkable how ideas that seem brilliant when floating around in one's brain end up looking vague and imprecise when committed to paper.) Another way to review would be to jot down a brief outline of the points that the essay would cover, and talk them through orally. Jotting an outline down before beginning an essay is always a good practice.

Evaluating Evidence (Maps, Illustrations, and Charts). Each Critical Thinking section begins with questions asking for evaluation or analysis of the text's illustrative material. As authors, we feel strongly that students, professors, and even the writers of many textbooks do not pay close enough attention to the materials that accompany the core narrative. We have included the maps, graphs, and illustrations not merely as window dressing but as ways to make clearer the points in the text.

Primary Source. Each chapter concludes with a primary source excerpt that illustrates one of the chapter's themes. A *primary source* is one that has been written (or made, or left behind in some way) by historical subjects themselves. It could be a diary, a song, a last will and testament, or the sketch on the back of an envelope. Primary sources are the raw materials of history: those pieces of the puzzle from which all history books are pieced together. We include a selection of them in order to underline what a chancy business interpreting history is. The "lessons" history provides are usually not so evident in the primary sources as they are in a textbook. To understand a subject in depth, we must all become our own historians, going to the primary sources to put together the story for ourselves.

Obviously, in such a short space we can provide only a hint of what that process involves, just as in *Nation of Nations* we can sketch only the major outlines of American history. But in the text and Study Guide, we hope we have provided enough of both the sinews and the savor of the historian's task so that you may wish to continue your own explorations of history. Like it or not, the events shaping this teeming nation of nations have also defined and shaped us, and we can look to our future more intelligibly the better we understand the contours of our past.

OLD WORLD, NEW WORLDS

KEYS TO THE CHAPTER

LEARNING OBJECTIVES

When you have finished studying this chapter, you should be able to:

1. Describe the character of Indian cultures and western European society in the fifteenth century, identifying comparisons and contrasts.

2. Explain why western Europeans were able to establish colonies across the Atlantic during the early modern period.

3. Describe the Spanish empire in America and discuss its impact on European development.

4. Explain the significance of the Protestant Reformation and its relationship to western Europe's expansion.

THE CHAPTER IN PERSPECTIVE

Early modern Europe emerged from its isolation and localism during the Middle Ages by conquering the world's oceans—opening direct contact and commerce with Africa and Asia and rediscovering America. Before the end of the fourteenth century, western Europeans had relied on the mariners and merchants of the Muslim world for their access to the trade and technology of Africa and Asia. But during the fifteenth century, western Europeans mastered the sea, carved out new sea routes to Africa and Asia, and laid claim to the Americas. The results of those efforts at exploration and discovery transformed western Europe from a backward society into a major world power.

OVERVIEW

The story of European exploration and discovery in the fifteenth and sixteenth centuries starts with the international fishing community off Newfoundland. The tales traded by these ordinary seamen and traders featured the Portuguese explorations of the coast of Africa and their charting of a new route to Asia, the efforts of John Cabot to find a northwest passage to the Orient, and, of course, Columbus's discovery of America.

The Meeting of Europe and America

Encounters with the Americas occurred because of Europeans' conquest of the high seas, which in turn was part of a larger technological, economic, demographic, and cultural transformation. The outward reach began with the successful voyages of the Portuguese into the Atlantic in the late 1300s. By the early 1400s they had established sugar plantations on the Atlantic islands worked by enslaved Africans. The Portuguese also initiated a trade with West Africa. By the end of the century their explorers had rounded the tip of that continent and opened a direct commerce with India.

The Spanish laid claim to the Americas, led by the discovery of an Italian mariner, Christopher Columbus.

Early North American Cultures

Asian migrants crossed the Bering Strait to Alaska many millennia before 1492. When Europeans first arrived in the Americas, these Indian cultures were numerous and diverse.

The Aztec economy and society encountered by Spanish explorers was similar in some respects to that of sixteenth-century Europe. One crucial difference, however, was that Aztec expansionism did not take the form of exploration and colonization across the seas.

The European Background of American Colonization

Conditions in late medieval Europe bred a sense of crisis mixed with a sense of possibility. Life was uncertain and often violent. The economic and political evolution concentrated investment capital in the hands of merchants, financiers, and landlords. Population growth put pressure on a limited supply of land. Political authority became concentrated in nation-states. All these changes, coupled with advances in maritime technology, allowed Europeans to push back the ocean frontier and to support overseas settlement.

Spain's Empire in the New World

Spain took the lead in exploring and colonizing the Americas. Conquistadors like Hernando Cortes supplanted native societies as the new overlords of Central and South America. Technological superiority, divisions within Indian empires, and the devastation of native populations by European diseases made the Spanish conquest easier.

Spanish monarchs replaced the conquistadors with their own rule through an elaborate civil and ecclesiastical bureaucracy. The empire that developed in the sixteenth century rested largely on the coerced labor of natives and imported Africans. It proved enormously profitable. That wealth, in turn, made Spain the dominant power in Europe.

The Reformation in Europe

While Catholic Spain developed its American empire, the Protestant Reformation transformed western Europe, and added a new dimension to the ensuing competition for empire. Protestant reformers criticized the nature and teachings of the Roman Catholic Church. They said that men and women were saved not by good works but through divine grace alone. Protestants also stressed the ability of each individual to read and understand the will of God as revealed in the Bible. By the reign of Elizabeth, Protestantism was established in England, although an impatient minority wanted to "purify" it further.

England's Entry into the New World

Protestant attacks on Roman Catholicism won both zealous followers and determined opponents, triggering a series of bloody religious wars. Young Englishmen found adventure in these religious conflicts, as well as in England's effort to conquer and colonize Ireland.

Many veterans of the Irish campaigns turned their attention to North America in the 1570s and 1580s. The threat Spain posed to English economic and military security encouraged Elizabeth I to challenge Spain more aggressively. English merchants and gentlemen, in search of new markets and new land, lent increasing support to colonization schemes as well. A series of failed efforts at colonization paved the way for renewed English expansionism in the seventeenth century.

KEY EVENTS

ca. 50,000-25,000 B.P.	*First Asian penetration of the Americas:* initial human settlement of the two continents
ca. 1300	*Rise of the Aztec empire:* in present-day Mexico
1271-1295	*Marco Polo travels to China from Italy*
1347	*First outbreak of the Black Death:* Europe's population declines drastically
1420s	*Portuguese settlements in the Atlantic Islands:* western Europe first penetrates its ocean frontier

1492	*Columbus discovers America*
1497	*John Cabot discovers Newfoundland*
1498	*Da Gama reaches India:* Europe opens a direct trade with the Far East
1517	*Luther posts his 95 theses:* Protestant Reformation begins
1519-1522	*Magellan circumnavigates the globe*
1521	*Tenochtitlán surrenders to Cortes:* Aztec empire falls
1540	*Discovery of silver in Mexico and Peru:* Spain vastly enriched by its overseas empire
1558	*Elizabeth I becomes queen of England*
1565	*England begins its conquest of Ireland:* the first effort at colonization by England
1584-1590	*Roanoke voyages:* England makes its first effort at colonization in North America

REVIEW QUESTIONS

MULTIPLE CHOICE

1. By the 1550s, English, French, Portuguese, and Spanish fishermen could be found fishing, trading, and relating sailing stories annually in:
   a. New York City.
   b. Roanoke Island.
   c. Newfoundland.
   d. San Francisco Bay.
   (p. 5)

2. In the 1400s, Prince Henry the Navigator sponsored voyages and trained shipmasters, hoping to bring new wealth and glory for:
   a. England.
   b. Portugal.
   c. Spain.
   d. Holland.
   (p. 6)

3. Which of the following is TRUE about Christopher Columbus?
    a. Unlike most educated Europeans of his day, he believed the earth was round.
    b. Monarchs of several countries made competitive bids to win the right to sponsor his first voyage.
    c. He named the "New World" after his brother-in-law, Amerigo Vespucci.
    d. Despite four voyages across the Atlantic, he failed to achieve his original objective.
    (pp. 8-10)

4. Although misnamed "Indians" by Columbus, the Native Americans in the Western Hemisphere were the descendants of Asians who came to the "New World" thousands of years before the Europeans by:
    a. crossing a temporary land bridge across the Bering Strait from Siberia to Alaska.
    b. sailing large ships from islands in the central Pacific.
    c. sailing small, simple boats from what is now China and Indonesia.
    d. migrating across Antarctica, then moving further north.
    (p. 10)

5. One major difference between Aztec civilization and that of the Spanish was that the Aztecs:
    a. did not practice slavery.
    b. did not possess a written language.
    c. had no urban centers of great size.
    d. did not expand their territory by sailing across oceans.
    (p. 14)

6. Aztecs were known for all of the following EXCEPT:
    a. participating in a lively trade in various goods.
    b. engaging in mass human sacrifice to the Sun God.
    c. having friendly alliances with neighboring tribes.
    d. a high susceptibility to smallpox and other diseases brought by the Spanish.
    (pp. 13-20)

7. Bartolome de las Casas was best known for:
    a. speaking out against the Spanish exploitation of the natives.
    b. leading the Spanish conquest of the Incas in present-day Peru.
    c. devising the encomienda system.
    d. initiating the Protestant Reformation in heavily Catholic Spain.
    (p. 21)

8. Martin Luther believed that:
   a. indulgences provided a democratic way to open salvation to all.
   b. only the so-called "elect" were predestined to go to heaven.
   c. the pope should have granted Henry VIII a marriage annulment.
   d. every Christian had the power claimed by Catholic priests.
   (pp. 22-23)

9. As something of a model for later colonization across the Atlantic, Queen Elizabeth sponsored efforts by English Protestants to settle and subdue predominantly Catholic:
   a. Holland.
   b. Ireland.
   c. Scotland.
   d. Sweden.
   (p. 26)

10. Sir Humphrey Gilbert:
    a. succeeded in establishing the first permanent English settlement in North America.
    b. failed in his attempt to establish the first permanent English settlement in North America.
    c. was jailed by King James I.
    d. led the Puritan movement in England.
    (pp. 27-29)

11. The "Lost Colony" of Roanoke Island was located off the coast of:
    a. Newfoundland.
    b. Cape Cod.
    c. present-day North Carolina.
    d. present-day Florida.
    (p. 29)

12. King James I wanted to:
    a. put an end to English efforts to settle North America.
    b. increase England's power and wealth by imitating in North America what the Spanish had done in Mexico and much of South America.
    c. promote his ideals of democracy, free enterprise, and Catholicism throughout the world, and especially in the "New World."
    d. treat the native peoples living in North America with more respect and compassion than the Spanish had done in South America.
    (p. 31)

COMPLETION

By the time Columbus first sailed across the Atlantic in 1492, Europe's old difficulties with _____ had arisen again. This demographic problem, along with changes in technology, politics, and religion, led European nations to venture out in search of new lands and goods. _____ took the early lead, as Prince Henry the Navigator sponsored the search for _____, a priest rumored to rule a Christian kingdom beyond the Muslim lands in Africa and Asia. _____ eventually become the dominant power during the late fifteenth and sixteenth centuries, after _____ sponsored Columbus in an effort to even the competition with the Portuguese. The Spanish conquistadors defeated Moctezuma and the _____, helped greatly by the various diseases they unwittingly brought with them from Europe. Spain ruled its empire primarily through oppression of the natives, using systems such as _____ to gain wealth for themselves and the Spanish crown. One reason Spain met with little interference in the Americas from other European nations was the _____ upheaval. Reformers such as Martin Luther and John Calvin led attacks on the Catholic church, rejecting practices such as the selling of _____ and promoting salvation based on _____ alone, as well as the belief that God had already decided which people would enter the kingdom of heaven, also known as _____. After successes in Ireland and the consolidation of power at home, England's _____ became more amenable to the idea of English expansion overseas, particularly after the Spanish sacking of the city of _____. However, the initial efforts of English explorers such as Frobisher and _____ failed, as did the colonization efforts at Roanoke Island by_____.

IDENTIFICATION

You should be able to describe the following key terms, concepts, individuals, and places, and explain their significance:

Terms and Concepts

Agricultural revolution	Privateers
Encomienda	Reconquista
Black Legend	Indulgences
Protestant Reformation	Doctrine of calling
Quadrant	Black Death
Price Revolution	El Dorado
Justification by faith alone	Conquistadore

Individuals and Places

Marco Polo	Prince Henry of Portugal
Bartholomeu Dias	Vasco da Gama
Arawaks	Amerigo Vespucci
Pueblo Indians	Ferdinand Magellan
Hernando de Soto	Moctezuma
Bartolomé de Las Casas	Martin Luther
John Calvin	Puritans
Martin Frobisher	Francis Drake
Francisco Vasquez de Coronado	

MAP IDENTIFICATION

On the map, label or shade in the following places. In a sentence, note their significance to the chapter. (For reference, consult the map on page 19 of *Nation of Nations*.)

1. Aztec Empire
2. Mesoamerica
3. The Spanish Main
4. The West Indies
5. The Caribbean Sea

ESSAY

1. Discuss the conditions that encouraged early modern Europeans to undertake voyages of exploration and discovery. What factor was most essential in encouraging them?

2. Describe the conditions under which indigenous American cultures became more complex and elaborate.

3. Characterize the Protestant Reformation as both an ecclesiastical revolution and a response to social conditions.

4. How does the Black Death (and its impact in Europe) compare to the impact on Native Americans of the diseases brought over by the Europeans?

5. You are a 40-year-old Aztec basketmaker. Describe how the arrival of the Spanish, some 20 years ago, has affected you and your community.

North, Central and South America

CRITICAL THINKING

EVALUATING EVIDENCE (MAPS AND ILLUSTRATIONS)

1. What does the scope of English and French exploration shown by the map on page 9 indicate about the evolution of relations between those nations with Spain in the sixteenth century?

2. What was the dominant mode of subsistence among North American Indian tribes, as indicated by the map on page 11?

3. What is the significance of the ivory mask fashioned by a West African artist (shown on page 7)? What does the mask indicate about the African perception of the Portuguese?

PRIMARY SOURCE: John Cabot's Discovery of Newfoundland[*]

Raimondo de Raimondi de Soncino, an Italian diplomat living in England, sent the Duke of Milan this delightful report of the excitement in London after John Cabot returned in 1497. Cabot had crossed the Atlantic and reached the northern tip of Newfoundland, which he believed to be eastern Asia.

> *Perhaps amid the numerous occupations of your Excellency, it may not weary you to hear how his Majesty here has gained a part of Asia, without a stroke of the sword. There is in this Kingdom a man of the people, Messer Zoane Caboto [John Cabot] by name, of kindly wit and a most expert mariner. Having observed that the sovereigns first of Portugal and then of Spain had occupied unknown islands, he decided to make a similar acquisition for his Majesty. After obtaining patents that the effective ownership of what he might find should be his, though reserving the rights of the Crown, he committed himself to fortune in a little ship, with eighteen persons. He started from Bristol, a port on the west of this kingdom, passed Ireland, which is still further west, and then bore towards the north, in order to sail to the east....After having wandered for some time he at length arrived at the mainland, where he hoisted the royal standard, and took possession for the king here; and after taking certain tokens he returned.*

> *This Messer Zoane, as a foreigner and a poor man, would not have obtained credence, had it not been that his companions, who are practically all English and from Bristol, testified that he spoke the truth. This Messer Zoane has the description of the world in a map, and also in a solid sphere, which he has made, and shows where he has been....These same English, his companions, say that they could bring so many fish that this kingdom would have no further need of Iceland.... But Messer Zoane has his mind set upon even greater things, because he proposes to keep along the coast from the place at which he touched, more and more towards the east, until he reaches an island which he calls Cipango...where he believes that all the spices of the world have their origin, as well as the jewels....*

---

[*] From *Calendar of State Papers, Milan* (1912), 18 December, 1497.

He tells this in such a way, and makes everything so plain, that I also feel compelled to believe him....Before very long they say that his Majesty will equip some ships, and in addition he will give them all the malefactors, and they will go to that country and form a colony. By means of this they hope to make London a more important mart for spices than Alexandria. The leading men in this enterprise are from Bristol, and great seamen, and now they know where to go, say that the voyage will not take more than a fortnight, if they have good fortune after leaving Ireland. I have also spoken with a Burgundian, one of Messer Zoane's companions, who corroborates everything. He wants to go back, because the Admiral, which is the name they give to Messer Zoane, has given him an island. He has given another to his barber, a Genoese by birth, and both consider themselves counts, while my lord the Admiral esteems himself at least a prince.

Questions

1. What was de Soncino's view of Cabot? Of Cabot's ambitions? Did he believe Cabot's story of discovery?

2. According to de Soncino, what prompted Cabot's explorations?

3. What was the role of the West Country men of Bristol in Cabot's successes? What did the Bristol men hope to gain by Cabot's discoveries?

THE FIRST CENTURY OF SETTLEMENT IN THE COLONIAL SOUTH

KEYS TO THE CHAPTER

LEARNING OBJECTIVES

When you have finished studying this chapter, you should be able to:

1. Trace the general process of colony building in the seventeenth century southern colonies: from initial founding through episodes of social crisis to stable, gentry-dominated societies.

2. Describe relations between colonists and the Powhatan confederacy of the Chesapeake and outline the objectives of both groups.

3. Explain the ways in which the introduction of staple crop economies—tobacco, sugar, and rice—transformed the societies of the Chesapeake, the Caribbean, and South Carolina.

4. Describe and explain why slavery became the dominant labor system in the southern colonies and how it affected the social and political order.

5. Contrast Spanish settlements in the Southwest with the British colonies of the Southeast.

THE CHAPTER IN PERSPECTIVE

The utopian hopes that had inspired some sixteenth-century English promoters of colonization—Gilbert, Raleigh, and Hakluyt—faltered and quickly failed during the first century of English settlement. This failure was most starkly evident in the southern colonies; that is, in the Chesapeake, the Carolinas, and the Caribbean. Instead of becoming havens for the English poor and unemployed or models of interracial harmony, the southern colonies in the 1600s were weakened by disease, wracked by recurring conflicts with native Americans, and disrupted by the exploitation of poor whites and blacks alike by the masters of tobacco, sugar, and rice plantations. Many of the tragedies of Spanish colonization and England's conquest of Ireland were repeated in the British Caribbean and southern mainland.

OVERVIEW

Just as the English established their first outpost on Chesapeake Bay with a set of goals and strategies in mind, so too the native Indians, under their leader Powhatan, pursued their own aims and interests. Powhatan used the "inferior" English newcomers to advance his own longstanding objectives of consolidating his political authority and fending off challenges from the Piedmont tribes.

English Society on the Chesapeake

But after Powhatan's death, the English presence proved more likely to threaten than to support these objectives. The European theory of mercantilism encouraged colonies as a means to achieving national self-sufficiency through international trade. If a colony could produce a commodity that would enrich investors and enhance royal revenues, it was highly prized. With the beginning of a boom in tobacco, an increasing number of white settlers came to Virginia, the vast majority as indentured servants.

The spread of English plantations encroached on tribal lands. Hostilities erupted between whites and Indians. Appalling casualties resulted, as well as a determination, on the part of the English, to destroy the "savage" Indians. Another casualty of the conflict was the Virginia Company itself.

When the price of tobacco leveled off, a more coherent social and political order took shape in Virginia and in its neighbor and rival, Maryland. England did little to direct the development in the Chesapeake region because it became distracted by domestic political upheavals that culminated in a Civil War. With the restoration of the monarchy in 1660, however, Charles II launched a more consistent colonial policy.

Chesapeake Society in Crisis

The Navigation Acts, designed to regulate colonial trade in ways that, following mercantilist theory, benefited England, only made worse the forces already shaking Chesapeake society. Freed servants and small planters found their opportunities shrinking. Hostilities with the Indians resumed. Political and religious rivalries deepened tensions. Two uprisings resulted.

A shift to using and exploiting African slave labor finally eased the strife within white society. The presence of imported Africans—legally coerced and distinct— unified whites of all classes and religions. Improved economic prospects for whites strengthened this consensus based on race. A new Chesapeake "gentry" encouraged the development of a subordinate and deferential (but prosperous) small-planter class.

From the Caribbean to the Carolinas

A booming sugar economy also transformed the Caribbean into a slave-based plantation society. Land scarcity on English Barbados fostered settlement of South Carolina.

Much like other proprietary colonies, South Carolina suffered from chronic political factions. Social instability, the result of ethnic and religious diversity, and high mortality rates compounded the unrest. Worsening Indian relations resulted in the devastating Yamasee War in 1715, which brought the colony to the brink of dissolution and ended proprietary rule.

Now a royal colony, South Carolina prospered by exporting rice and indigo. Greater social and political harmony ensued, mainly because whites unified against the threat posed by the black slave majority. The founding of Georgia formed a buffer between South Carolina and Spanish Florida.

The Spanish Borderlands

While the English colonies in southern North America were taking shape, the Spanish pushed northward into the American Southwest, scattering military garrisons and cattle ranches throughout the region. To incorporate Indians into colonial society as docile servants and pious farmers and artisans, the Spanish relied on missions staffed by Dominican and Franciscan priests. Like the English in the Chesapeake and the Carolinas, the Spanish in the Southwest encountered sustained resistance to their expansionism from Indian cultures.

In sum, dreams of empire or independence cherished by red, white, and black inhabitants suffered disappointment and sometimes disaster during the seventeenth century.

KEY EVENTS

late 1500s	*Formation of Powhatan's Confederacy*
1604	*First English settlements in the Caribbean*
1607	*English settle Jamestown:* first permanent English colony on the mainland of North America
1610	*Spanish found Santa Fe:* establishing a capital for their empire in the present-day southwestern United States
1619	*First African-Americans arrive in Virginia*
1620s	*Tobacco boom in Virginia:* the beginning of a monoculture in the Chesapeake

1622	*White-Indian warfare in Virginia:* enormous casualties weaken both sides
1624	*Virginia becomes a royal colony*
1632	*Calvert founds Maryland:* Virginians resent competition
1640s	*The sugar boom begins in the Caribbean:* slaves become more numerous and land more scarce
1660	*Parliament passes the first of the Navigation Acts*
1669	*First permanent white settlement in South Carolina*
1676	*Bacon's Rebellion in Virginia:* civil war engulfs the colony
1680	*Pueblo Revolt in New Mexico:* massive Indian resistance
ca. 1700	*Rice boom begins in South Carolina:* slave importations increase dramatically
1715	*Yamasee uprising in South Carolina:* native Indian tribes push white settlement back to Charleston
1730	Chartering of Georgia

REVIEW QUESTIONS

MULTIPLE CHOICE

1. Powhatan reacted to the English settlement of Jamestown by:
   a. defeating the settlers and removing nearly every trace of them.
   b. moving his tribe further west toward the Appalachians.
   c. establishing a joint tobacco-raising cooperative with the English.
   d. trading food to the English in exchange for guns and other supplies that would help the Pamunkeys subdue rival tribes.
   (pp. 33-35)

2. Mercantilism is best understood as the:
   a. rise of the merchant class and their demand for a less powerful monarchy.
   b. state regulation and protection of commerce to enrich the nation by exporting more than importing.
   c. movement away from state regulation of commerce to allow the free market to determine trade.
   d. practice of using indentured servants to provide relatively cheap labor in colonial enterprises.
   (p. 36)

3. The Jamestown settlement was established as a:
  a. joint stock company seeking to make money.
  b. religious experiment led by Puritans.
  c. humanitarian effort to relieve London's overcrowding.
  d. trading post to sell food to the Indians.
  (pp. 36-37)

4. Which of the following is NOT true about the settlement of Jamestown and the entire Chesapeake region in the seventeenth century?
  a. Men outnumbered women by roughly 6 to 1.
  b. Most of those who came were from England's wealthiest families, as they were the only ones who could afford passage.
  c. Most who came were relatively young, with a high percentage from the 15- to 24-year-old age group.
  d. Life expectancy was poor at first but improved over time as food supplies increased.
  (pp. 38-42)

5. Which of the following is NOT true about the founding of Maryland?
  a. It began as a proprietary colony, founded by Catholic aristocrats.
  b. Virginians resented the economic competition.
  c. The colony quickly established religious freedom for all.
  d. Land was provided rent free.
  (p. 41)

6. The Navigation Acts were examples of:
  a. early self-rule by the colonial assemblies.
  b. the growing disinterest by the English government about affairs in the American colonies.
  c. mercantilism.
  d. the decline of mercantilism.
  (pp. 42-43)

7. Bacon's Rebellion:
  a. was a successful effort by wealthy Protestant planters to remove the Catholic proprietary government from power.
  b. so angered royal authorities that they dispatched troops to burn down the city of Jamestown.
  c. led to the formation of the Virginia House of Burgesses, the first colonial attempt at self-government.
  d. reflected the deep resentment by those who did not have political and economic power of those who did.
  (pp. 43-44)

8. African slaves became a more popular source of labor in the Chesapeake after 1680 because of all of the following EXCEPT:

 a. the initial investment for slaves was cheaper than for indentured servants.

 b. masters would have title to any children of slaves as well.

 c. the growth of African slavery helped to unite poorer and wealthier whites in racial solidarity.

 d. the growth of the slave trade.

 (pp. 45-47)

9. The "middle passage" referred to:

 a. the 5,000-mile journey across the Atlantic endured by enslaved Africans aboard tightly packed ships.

 b. the transformation of African labor in the English colonies from temporary servitude to lifelong slavery.

 c. laws enacted to place severe limits on the rights of Africans.

 d. the payment of trans-Atlantic ship fare in exchange for an "indenture" of several years' labor.

 (pp. 46-47)

10. The number of settlers and slaves grew dramatically in Barbados and other Caribbean islands after 1640, when the cash crop became:

 a. tobacco.

 b. sugar.

 c. bananas.

 d. cotton.

 (pp. 51-52)

11. James Oglethorpe and the others who founded Georgia envisioned it as a place that would:

 a. offer religious freedom for all.

 b. be a near utopia of small farmers.

 c. provide an opportunity for a new aristocracy of landed nobles in the English colonies.

 d. protect Florida colonists from attacks by the Spanish or Indian tribes.

 (pp. 56-57)

12. In 1680, the Spanish were driven out of New Mexico for more than a decade due to:

 a. the outbreak of the plague.

 b. defeat in the Yamasee War.

 c. the Great Pueblo Revolt.

 d. Coode's Rebellion.

 (p. 60)

COMPLETION

In 1606, King James I granted a charter to the _____. The next year, the company established the first permanent English settlement at _____. The first years of the colony, like those of many southern colonies to follow, were marked by instability and high rates of _____. After more than a decade of failures, the settlement finally began to thrive after the introduction of _____. When Maryland was founded in 1632, Virginians disliked the new colony not only because of its status as an economic competitor but also because it became a haven for _____. By the middle of the seventeenth century, both of these Chesapeake colonies began shifting the focus of their labor systems away from _____ and toward _____. The unrest of the small planters furthered this trend, particularly after _____ in 1676. After 1680, most of the Chesapeake slaves had to endure a trip across the Atlantic called the _____. Caribbean colonies had a high demand for slaves as well because of their success in marketing _____. Some of the immigrants to Barbados moved to the mainland and helped form the colony of _____ in 1669. Georgia, established by _____ in 1732, provided a buffer from the Spanish, who had formed a permanent colony at _____ as far back as 1565. The Spanish also formed a colony in New Mexico in 1598, but it had many disputes with the Indians, culminating in the _____ of 1680, which drove the Spanish out for over a decade.

IDENTIFICATION

You should be able to describe the following key terms, concepts, individuals, and places and explain their significance.

Terms and Concepts

Powhatan Confederacy	Navigation Acts
Royal African Company	Quitrents
Coode's Rebellion	Virginia Company of London
Yamasee War	Mission
Fundamental	Constitutions
Headrights	English Civil War
Restoration	Proprietary government
House of Burgesses	Bacon's Rebellion
Middle Passage	Great Pueblo Revolt
Mercantilism	Indentured servant

Individuals and Places

Captain John Smith
Calvert family
James I
Charles II
General James Oglethorpe
Santa Fe Popé

John Rolfe
Oliver Cromwell
Charles I
William Berkeley
St. Augustine

MAP IDENTIFICATION

On the map, label or shade in the following places. In a sentence, note their significance to the chapter. (For reference, consult the map on page 42 of *Nation of Nations*.)

1. Chesapeake Bay
2. The Tidewater
3. The Piedmont
4. Territory encompassed by the Powhatan Confederacy
5. Jamestown

ESSAY

1. What was mercantilism? Why did the logic of mercantilist ideas encourage King James to grant a charter to the Virginia Company?

2. Discuss the causes of Bacon's Rebellion in Virginia. Compare and contrast the causes and character of that rebellion with the causes and character of Coode's Rebellion in Maryland.

3. Compare and contrast the Spanish treatment of native peoples in California and the Southwest with relations between Indians and English settlers in the colonial American Southeast.

4. How did the increased use of slavery actually help prevent continued internal crises and conflicts among the white settlers? In other words, how did slavery promote stability among the white colonists?

5. Explain why you, as a frontiersman in the 1670s, might have been willing to follow Bacon and rebel against the governor of Virginia.

Mid-Atlantic states

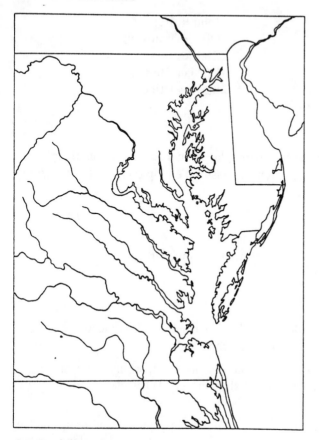

CRITICAL THINKING

EVALUATING EVIDENCE (MAPS AND ILLUSTRATIONS)

1. How does the map on page 42 help to explain what geographic factors shaped the extent of settlement in the Chesapeake by 1700?

2. What does the inset map of the Carolinas on page 54 suggest about the strategic opportunities—and dangers—of South Carolina?

3. The picture of early Jamestown (page 37) shows that settlement as a heavily palisaded fort. What factors besides the fear of Indian attack dictated the military character of early Jamestown?

PRIMARY SOURCE: White and Black Laborers in the Early Chesapeake[*]

A number of bound laborers, apprehended as they attempted to escape from their master's plantation, received the following sentences for their crime. The excerpt is from the legal records of early Virginia.

> July 22nd, 1640. Whereas complaint has been made to this Board by Capt. William Pierce, Esqr., that six of his servants and a negro of Mr. Reginald's has plotted to run away unto the Dutch plantation from their said masters, and did assay to put the same in Execution upon Saturday night, being the 8th day July, 1640, ... [and did take] the skiff of the said Capt. William Pierce, their master, and corn, powder and shot and guns to accomplish their said purposes, which said persons sailed down in the said skiff to Elizabeth river, where they were taken and brought back again, the court taking the same into consideration as a dangerous precedent for the future time (if left unpunished), did order that Christopher Miller, a dutchman (a prime agent in the business), should receive the punishment of whipping, and to have thirty stripes and so be burnt in the cheek with the letter R and to work with a shackle on his legg for one whole year and longer if said master shall see cause, and after his full time of service is Expired with his said master to serve the colony for seven whole years, and the said Peter Milcocke to receive thirty stripes and to be Burnt in the cheek with the letter R, and after his term of service is Expired with his said master to serve the colony for three years, and the said Richard Cockson, after his full time Expired with his master, to serve the colony for two years and a half, and the said Richard Hill to remain upon his good behavior untill the next offence, and the said Andrew Noxe to receive thirty stripes, and the said John Williams, a dutchman and a chirurgeon [surgeon] after his full time of service is Expired with his master, to serve the colony for seven years, and Emanuel, the Negro, to receive thirty stripes and to be burnt in the cheek with the letter R and to work in shackles one year or more as his master shall see cause....

[*] From *Decisions of the General Court*, 1640, reprinted in *The Virginia Magazine of History and Biography* (Vol. 5, 1897-1898), 236-37.

Questions

1. What does the wording of the document suggest about the awareness of ethnic and racial differences among early Virginians?

2. What does the document suggest about relations between servants and slaves in early Virginia?

3. Did differences in punishment correspond to ethnic or racial differences?

4. Why was the act of running away seen as a "dangerous precedent" deserving of serious punishment? What does that indicate about the court's perception of the social order in early Virginia?

THE FIRST CENTURY OF SETTLEMENT IN THE COLONIAL NORTH

KEYS TO THE CHAPTER

LEARNING OBJECTIVES

When you have finished studying this chapter, you should be able to:

1. Contrast the founding of the Puritan colonies in New England and the middle colonies, including a definition of a proprietary colony.

2. Explain why the early New England colonies were characterized by greater social stability than either the southern or middle colonies.

3. Explain how the legacy of the Reformation shaped the settlement of Puritan New England, Quaker Pennsylvania, and French Canada.

4. Compare and contrast relations between white settlers and Indians in New England, the Middle Colonies, and French Canada and, referring to Chapter 2, in the South and the Spanish Southwest as well.

5. Explain the significance of the Glorious Revolution in America.

THE CHAPTER IN PERSPECTIVE

As plantation societies took shape in the South, colonies of a much different character were developing in New England, New York, New Jersey, and Pennsylvania. Northern colonial societies constituted a dramatic counterpoint to the fragile, fragmented cultures of the Chesapeake, the Carolinas, and the Caribbean. The southern colonies were socially volatile and politically unstable, dominated by the quest for profit and divided by sharp racial and class antagonisms. To the north a healthier climate, a different economic base, and strong religious influences contributed to the emergence of more coherent societies.

OVERVIEW

Religion played a crucial role in shaping northern colonial settlement. In Canada, French Catholic missionaries, especially the Jesuits, helped to win acceptance among the native Indians for the few French soldiers, traders, and settlers there—whose interest was in trade more than land. At the same time, the impact of Protestantism in

England helped in motivating the settlement of Puritan New England, and later the Quaker exodus to Pennsylvania.

The Founding of New England

As the French slowly established a presence in Canada, radical Puritans—followers of John Calvin—fled persecution and "corruption" in England, planting settlements between Maine and Long Island. The first New England settlers, the Separatists or "Pilgrims," were humble English farmers and craftspeople who first sought refuge in the Netherlands. Concern for their children prompted them to found the Plymouth colony in 1620.

A larger and more important wave of Puritan migration first reached the shores of what became the colony of Massachusetts Bay in 1630. Led by John Winthrop, these Puritan migrants were wealthier and more prominent than the Pilgrim Separatists. They differed, too, in still believing the Church of England could be purified from within. They wanted to make their settlement a model for social and religious reform back in England.

New England Communities

The New England colonies were notable for their similarities. These included rapid population growth through natural increase, tight-knit communities committed to stability and order, patriarchal families, reliance on subsistence agriculture and widespread land ownership, a rough economic equality, and an absence of bound labor.

Strengthening the stability of early New England society were the shared commitment to Puritan, or Congregational, churches (whose members had to demonstrate a "converted" heart and life), and a strong tradition of self-government at both the town and colony level. In all of these respects, New England contrasted strikingly with the early American South.

Early New England did not lack conflict. Devout New Englanders could fight fiercely over theological disagreements. On occasion, tension between white and Indian settlements erupted into violent confrontations.

The Middle Colonies

The Middle Colonies shared with New England comparable agrarian economies, systems of free labor, and patterns of rapid population growth. Unlike New England, however, they had proprietary governments, such as Maryland and South Carolina. Representative government was therefore weaker, and civic life was more embattled—a situation compounded by ethnic and religious diversity.

In New York, Dutch Calvinist settlers were joined by English Anglicans and Puritans, French Huguenots, Portuguese Jews, Scandinavian Lutherans, and African-Americans, both slave and free. New Jersey, granted to a pair of proprietors who divided their holding, was even more complicated.

Relations between whites and Indians in the Middle Colonies also developed differently. While the Puritans sought to subdue the New England tribes, New Yorkers conciliated the powerful league of the Iroquois in order to maintain a competitive edge over the French for the fur trade. And for many decades, Quaker Pennsylvanians coexisted peaceably with the Lenni Lenapes.

Pennsylvania's Quakers practiced tolerance toward not only Native Americans but also religious dissenters. They hoped to create a religious utopia based on remarkably egalitarian ideals. Pennsylvania's economy grew rapidly, anchored by the trade flowing through the thriving port town of Philadelphia. Yet prosperous, religious Pennsylvania still was rent by political strife.

Adjustment to Empire

Charles II and James II's attempts to centralize England's American empire created serious disruptions of political life in every northern colony except Pennsylvania. The crown's experiment in centralization, the Dominion of New England, ended with the Glorious Revolution in 1688: James II was replaced by William and Mary. New England weathered these years of political instability without severe internal turmoil. New Yorkers, however, responded with violence and vicious political infighting.

The dismantling of the Dominion greatly reduced tensions between England and its colonies. For more than half a century, English monarchs gave up efforts to impose a strict, centralized administration on America. The virtual self-rule enjoyed by the colonies reflected the reality that these outposts of English civilization had matured into firmly rooted societies.

KEY EVENTS

late 1500s	*Formation of the League of the Iroquois*
1535	*Cartier discovers the St. Lawrence:* his efforts open the way for France to colonize North America
1608	*Champlain founds Quebec on the St. Lawrence*
1620	*Pilgrims land at Plymouth:* first English settlement north of Jamestown
1624	*Dutch found New Netherlands*

1630	*Winthrop fleet arrives at Massachusetts Bay:* triggers a mass Puritan emigration to New England
1637	*Pequot War:* the English decimate native tribes
1642-1648	*English Civil War:* the Puritans take control of England's government
1660	*English monarchy restored:* Charles II becomes king
1664	*New Netherlands becomes English New York; Founding of New Jersey*
1675-76	*Metacomet's War:* the English wrest control of all New England from native Indian tribes
1681	*Founding of Pennsylvania:* a haven for Quakers
1685	*James II becomes king of England*
1686	*Dominion of New England established:* James II places all territory north of Pennsylvania under royal control
1688	*Glorious Revolution:* William and Mary become England's monarchs
1689	*Massachusetts Bay overthrows Andros; Leisler's Rebellion in New York*

REVIEW QUESTIONS

MULTIPLE CHOICE

1. The principal economic motive prompting French exploration and settlement in North America was the lucrative trade in:
   a. sugar.
   b. tobacco.
   c. furs.
   d. silver.
   (p. 64)

2. The principal goal of the early Puritans was to:
   a. emigrate and set up a separate country with no ties to England.
   b. help bring King James to power.
   c. reform English society and the Church of England.
   d. revive the Roman Catholic Church in England.
   (pp. 66-67)

3. The Mayflower Compact:
  a. was a royal charter from King James providing the Pilgrims the right to set up a colony in North America.
  b. provided for an alliance between the Pilgrims in Plymouth and the local Wampanoag Indians.
  c. set up a framework for Plymouth's colonial government in which all adult males could vote for local officials.
  d. was a petition asking King James to forbid non-Pilgrims from being allowed to immigrate to Plymouth colony.
  (p. 68)

4. During the so-called "Great Migration" from 1630-1642, most of those who arrived in Massachusetts Bay Colony were:
  a. not in sympathy with the Puritans and established their own churches throughout New England.
  b. poor agricultural peasants, overwhelmingly male, in search of cheap land.
  c. primarily farmers, artisans, and merchants who came to the "New World" in families.
  d. Pilgrims.
  (pp. 69-70)

5. Roger Williams was expelled from Massachusetts Bay Colony for:
  a. pushing for the separation of church and state.
  b. preaching a form of heresy known as "Antinomianism."
  c. establishing a house of prostitution in Boston.
  d. his refusal to pay church taxes and his outspoken atheistic ideas.
  (p. 74)

6. Which of the following is NOT true about Anne Hutchinson?
  a. Most ministers in Boston supported her religious zeal.
  b. Hutchinson believed that obedience to God's laws revealed nothing about the inward state of the soul.
  c. Many important merchant families strongly supported her.
  d. Many especially disliked her because she was an outspoken, assertive woman at a time when women were expected to have no public role.
  (p. 75)

7. Most of those accused of witchcraft in 1692 were women who:
    a. had sought and achieved elective office in the previous decade but had recently been defeated.
    b. were young, recent arrivals to the community.
    c. had joined the local Quaker meeting house.
    d. were middle-aged or older and regarded as unduly independent.
    (pp. 75-77)

8. The Iroquois:
    a. were a matrilineal society in which women wielded political as well as social influence.
    b. made constant war on settlers in New York.
    c. maintained close alliances with the neighboring tribes, seeking to prevent exploitation by colonists.
    d. were pacifists who denounced warfare as unnatural.
    (pp. 80-81)

9. The Society of Friends (or Quakers) believed that:
    a. only those who professed themselves to be Quakers could enter God's kingdom.
    b. all men and women shared equally in the "Light Within" and should be considered equal in society.
    c. a holy war against non-Quakers was inevitable, which led to their expulsion from Massachusetts Bay.
    d. certain men had been ordained by God to be community leaders and deserved complete respect and deference from all.
    (p. 82)

10. Leisler's Rebellion in New York in 1689:
    a. was a short-lived effort by the Dutch to reclaim from the English what had once been their colony.
    b. returned the colony to Dutch hands for nearly 50 years.
    c. was a bloody raid on an Indian settlement.
    d. reflected aftershocks of the Glorious Revolution in England over who would rule in the colonies.
    (p. 86)

11. Wider enforcement of the Navigation Acts was provided by Parliament in 1696 in order to:
 a. protect the colonists from overzealous customs collectors.
 b. discourage colonial smuggling and insure that colonial trade was channeled through England.
 c. protect colonial ships against pirates.
 d. insure that all ships were adequately equipped with navigational equipment to sail safely across the Atlantic Ocean.
 (pp. 86-87)

12. The English imperial policy from around 1700 on was to:
 a. immediately withdraw from oversight of colonial affairs.
 b. gradually withdraw from oversight of all colonial affairs.
 c. retain control over the colonies, but allow many decisions to be made by the colonies themselves.
 d. sharply increase their control over all affairs in the colonies.
 (pp. 86-87)

COMPLETION

Unlike in Southern colonies, many of the settlers in the northern part of North America during the seventeenth century were fleeing from _____ persecution, and they came as families and communities rather than as single settlers. The growth of these colonies was helped by the healthier _____ in the North, as well as by their early willingness to establish _____ governments. Conflicts did emerge, however, many concerning _____. Individuals such as Roger Williams and _____ were deemed _____ by Massachusetts and forced to flee to other settlements. _____ were particularly susceptible to charges of religious blasphemy; many were accused of being _____. The Middle Colonies were also burdened with conflicts. New Netherlands was particularly hampered by the cultural _____ of its inhabitants. Another complicating factor for this colony was the sustained power of the _____ tribe within the interior of the territory. Pennsylvanians had little trouble with the Indians because the practice of _____ led many colonists to treat the natives fairly. Conflicts further arose throughout the northern colonies, however, when James II formed the _____ in order to provide the crown with economic benefits. After he was exiled during the _____ of 1688, however, _____ and _____ relaxed the authority of the crown over the colonies, and by 1700 royal power was more apparent than real.

IDENTIFICATION

You should be able to describe the following key terms, concepts, individuals, and places and explain their significance.

Terms and Concepts

"Flying" mission
Predestination
Mayflower Compact
Great Migration
Antinomianism
Conversion
League of the Iroquois
Dominion of New England
Counterreformation
Jesuits
Lords of Trade and Plantations

Coureurs du bois
Separatism
Freemanship
Hierarchy
Town meeting
"Light Within"
Sachems and Sagamores
Matrilineal kinship
Glorious Revolution
Quakerism
Leisler's Rebellion

Individuals and Places

Samuel de Champlain
Samoset and Squanto
Archbishop William Laud
John Winthrop
Roger Williams
Mary Dyer
Metacomet
Lenni Lenapes
James II
Jacques Cartier

Quebec
Acadia
Congregationalists
Thomas Hooker
Anne Hutchinson
Pequots
New Netherlands
William Penn
Sir Edmund Andros
William and Mary

MAP IDENTIFICATION

On the map, label or shade in the following places. In a sentence, note their significance to the chapter. (For reference, consult the map on page 70 of *Nation of Nations*.)

1. Massachusetts
2. Connecticut
3. Rhode Island
4. Long Island
5. The centers of English settlement in the seventeenth century

New England

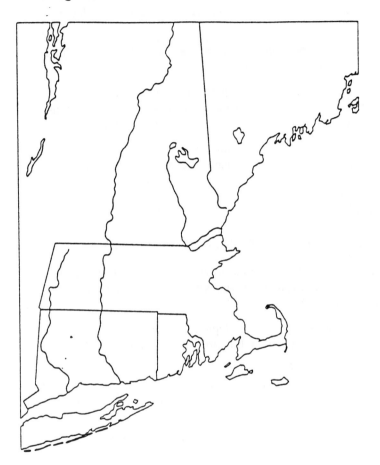

ESSAY

1. Compare the French motives for colonizing North America with those of the English.

2. What were the principal religious beliefs of the Puritans? What role did the Congregational church play in New England villages?

3. Contrast the settlement process of the Chesapeake and New England. How did these early migrations help to determine the initial character of these two colonial societies?

4. It could be argued that both religious and economic factors made it easier for the French than the English to coexist with Indian cultures. Discuss those factors and explain why you agree or disagree.

5. What does the text mean by ethnic and religious diversity in the Middle Colonies? Did that diversity differ from New England?

6. Explain how and why the beliefs and customs of both Puritans and Quakers challenged traditional English society. Why then did New England's Puritans persecute Quakers, since both groups were, after all, devout reformers?

7. You came to Massachusetts with your husband and family in 1632. Forty years later, you want to write to your sister in England describing things you have experienced in the "New World."

CRITICAL THINKING

EVALUATING EVIDENCE (MAPS AND ILLUSTRATIONS)

1. What does the inset map of Sudbury, Massachusetts, on page 70 suggest about the character of local life in New England? In what ways would the physical layout of towns like Sudbury influence social life?

2. Why did the Quakers condone the practice, depicted on page 76, of women preaching? Why didn't the Quakers, like the Puritans, interpret the biblical teachings of St. Paul as forbidding such a practice?

3. The picture on page 65 shows Indian converts to Christianity demonstrating ritual acts of humility typical of Catholic religious orders. Why would Catholics and Protestants advocate the virtues of self-denial while seeking to convert others to their faith? Should this be understood as contradictory or consistent with Christian ideals?

PRIMARY SOURCE: A Puritan View of the Migration to New England[*]

Edward Johnson, an artisan born in Canterbury, England, migrated to Boston in 1630. Ten years later he helped to found Woburn, Massachusetts, and remained one of its leading citizens. His history of early Massachusetts, entitled *Wonder-Working Providence of Sions Saviour in New England,* was published in London in 1654. Thomas Shepard, whose escape to New England Johnson described in this excerpt, was a minister being sought by English authorities because of his outspoken Puritan convictions.

---

[*] From Edward Johnson, *Wonder-Working Providence of Sions Saviour in New England* (164).

When England began to decline in Religion…and instead of purging out Popery, a farther compliance was sought not onely in vaine Idolatrous Ceremonies, but also in prophaning the Sabbath…in so much that the multitude of irreligious lascivious and popish affected persons spred the whole land like Grashoppers, in this very time Christ the glorious King of his Churches, raises an Army out of our English Nation for freeing his people from their long servitude under usurping Prelacy; and because every corner of England was filled with the fury of militant adversaries, Christ creates a New England to muster up the first of his Force in; Whose low condition, little number, and remotenesse of place made these adversaries triumph…but in this hight of their pride the Lord Christ brought sudden, and unexpected destruction upon them. Thus have you a touch of the time when this worke began.

*   *   *   *   *   *

Now my loving Reader, let mee lead thee by the hand to our Native Land…come with mee and behold the wonderous worke of Christ in preserving…that soule ravishing Minister Mr. Thomas Shepheard, who came this yeare to Yarmouth to ship for New England…in which time some persons eagerly hunting for Mr. Thomas Shepheard, began to plot (for apprehending him) with a Boy of sixteene or seventeene yeares of Age, who lived in the House where he Lodged to open the doore for them at a certaine houre in the night; But the Lord Christ, who is the Shepheard of Israel kept a more sure watch over his indeared servants, for thus it befell, the sweet words of grace falling from the lips of this Reverend and godly Mr. Thomas Shepheard in the hearing of the Boy (the Lords working withall) hee was perswaded this was an holy man of God, and therefore…with teares hee tells that on such a night hee had agreed to let in Men to apprehend the godly Preacher… [Shepheard], with the help of some well-affected persons was convay'd away…through a back Lane.…

But the Lord Christ intending to make his New England Souldiers the very wonder of this Age, brought [Shepheard] into greater straites, that this Wonder working Providence might the more appeare in his deliverance, for comming a shipboard…in little time after they were tossed and sore beaten with a contrary winde.…the Master, and other Sea men made a strange construction of the sore storme they met withall, saying, their Ship was bewitched, and therefore made use of the common Charme ignorant people use, nailing two red hot horseshoos to their maine mast. But assuredly it was the Lord Christ, who hath

*command both of Winds and Seas, and now would have his people
know he hath delivered, and will deliver from so great a death....*

Questions

1. What evidence from these passages indicates that Johnson was a Puritan settler of Massachusetts Bay and not a Plymouth Pilgrim?

2. What was Johnson's view of England at the time of the Puritan exodus? What did he mean by "Popery?"

3. What is the significance of the date and place of publication of Johnson's history?

4. Why did Johnson include the story of the horseshoe charm in his history? What does this episode indicate about Puritan attitudes toward magic?

5. What was Johnson's main purpose in writing this history?

THE MOSAIC OF
EIGHTEENTH-CENTURY AMERICA

KEYS TO THE CHAPTER

LEARNING OBJECTIVES

When you have finished studying this chapter, you should be able to:

1. Explain the evolving contest between the Indians, the French, and the British for supremacy and survival in North America.

2. Describe life on the eighteenth-century American frontier, in cities, and on plantations.

3. Explain the relationship among population growth, social diversity, and political division and instability in eighteenth-century America.

4. Explain the impact of the Enlightenment and the Great Awakening.

5. Describe colonial views of England and English views of the colonies in the middle of the eighteenth century.

THE CHAPTER IN PERSPECTIVE

A century of settlement produced a full-fledged, firmly rooted society on the mainland of British North America. But it was not a homogeneous society. Colonial society included a mixture of peoples, free and unfree, from different ethnic, racial, and religious backgrounds and without a common national identity or a common culture. They possessed diverse interests and economic pursuits. Their political fate remained in question as well, as the English, French, and Indians vied for control over the continent. The developments after 1700 intensified both social diversity and political uncertainty, resulting in increasing conflict, both internal and international.

OVERVIEW

The chapter provides three different portraits of eighteenth-century North America. Its most precise focus is on the growing diversity of peoples, interests, and outlooks—in the backcountry, the seaport, and the plantation slave community. It also contrasts British colonial society with the society of the parent country. Most broadly, it takes in the most far-reaching evidence of diversity—and conflict—in eighteenth-century North America: the international struggle for control of the continent waged by the French, the English, and native Indian tribes. Wars fought in both Europe and America between 1689 and 1748 culminated in the Seven Years' War.

Benjamin Franklin's 1754 Albany Plan would have provided for greater political coherence for the British North American empire, but the colonies rejected it, reflecting the jealous localism and social distinctiveness of eighteenth-century Americans.

Forces of Division

American population nearly doubled every 25 years—partly from accelerated immigration, partly from natural increase. The pressure of that expanding population pushed settlement westward and created communities that developed different interests and distinct cultures from those along the coast.

Most Americans on the move settled in the backcountry; some swelled the populations of major colonial seaports. The arrival of non-English immigrants and increasingly heavy slave importations only intensified continuing ethnic and sectional divisions. The most serious social and political conflict drew its strength from controversies between east and west, contests between colonies over boundaries, and quarrels over tenancy.

Slave Societies in the Eighteenth-Century South

The plantation districts of the eighteenth-century southern coast became regions of tension and conflict, too. As more and more Africans arrived, the black community was divided internally between native-born slaves and West African newcomers and was marked by various strategies of slave resistance. Differences among blacks lessened after about 1750. A distinctively African-American culture emerged, although black families remained vulnerable.

Enlightenment and Awakening in America

Differences in thought and belief both transcended local differences and compounded the tensions of racial, regional, and ethnic diversity.

While the Enlightenment prompted some American elites to conceive of a benevolent God of moralistic "rational Christianity," an even larger number of Americans embraced the evangelical Christianity preached by revivalists. The Great Awakening provided a common experience for many different folk from throughout the colonies. Yet their conversions also sharpened tensions.

Anglo-American Worlds of the Eighteenth Century

Despite their differences, a majority of white Americans shared a pride in their common English ancestry. Colonials revered the British constitutional system as providing the world's best and freest form of government.

Yet England was different from America. England's economy was more commercially and industrially developed. Its society was more urbanized and aristocratic, and hence had much greater extremes of rich and poor. Thus, an undercurrent of ambivalence characterized colonial attitudes toward England. Some Americans who crossed the Atlantic recognized that the English elite had purchased benefits for the few at a high social cost and expressed reservations about the economic and social inequality and corruption of English politics. Even so, American criticism of England in the middle of the eighteenth century was muted by the advantages that an imperial policy of benign neglect afforded.

Toward the Seven Years' War

1754 changed the imperial relationship. Leadership in both America and England faced a great climactic war for the empire, during which both the balance of power in North America and the nature of imperial administration would shift dramatically.

KEY EVENTS

1689-97	*King William's War (War of the League of Augsburg)*
1702-1713	*Queen Anne's War (War of the Spanish Succession):* the second war for empire between England and France
1739	*George Whitefield's first preaching tour in America:* initiates the first Great Awakening
	Stono Rebellion in South Carolina: slave insurrection
1744-48	*King George's War (War of the Austrian Succession):* the third war for empire between England and France
1754	*The Albany Congress:* failed to bring political unity
	Washington surrenders at Fort Necessity
1760-69	*South Carolina Regulation:* unrest in the backcountry
1763	*Paxton Boys' March:* unrest in Pennsylvania
1766-1771	*North Carolina Regulation:* sectional tension in the southern backcountry culminates in the Battle of Alamance, 1771

REVIEW QUESTIONS

MULTIPLE CHOICE

1. The opening story in the chapter deals with the Albany Congress, at which colonial representatives:
   - a. officially declared war on all Indian tribes except the Iroquois.
   - b. approved a Plan of Union for all the colonies to create "one general government" for British North America.
   - c. hotly debated Benjamin Franklin's proposal for gradual independence.
   - d. declared a temporary truce with the French in order to focus their military force against the Iroquois.

   (pp. 90-92)

2. During the early- and mid-1700s, immigration into the colonies:
   - a. slowed to a trickle, but the general population grew.
   - b. slowed to a trickle, and the general population leveled off.
   - c. grew tremendously, and the general population grew even more.
   - d. grew tremendously, but the general population grew only moderately.

   (p. 93)

3. Scotch-Irish and German immigrants were LEAST likely to immigrate to:
   - a. New England.
   - b. the Carolinas.
   - c. Pennsylvania.
   - d. Virginia.

   (p. 95)

4. The Paxton Boys' protest and the Regulation movements symbolized:
   - a. bitter opposition by the English colonists to German immigration.
   - b. growing conflicts between those who lived in the backcountry and those in a colony's eastern seaboard.
   - c. a rising discontent among the landless poor in seaports.
   - d. a growing concern for the plight of the Native Americans.

   (p. 96)

5. "Negro Election Day" was:
    a. a code phrase for public auctions of African slaves.
    b. an annual festival celebrated by African-Americans, similar to ones held in West Africa.
    c. established in most northern colonies for free Africans to cast legitimate votes for local offices.
    d. the date set by plantation owners for slaves to mediate grievances and disputes between themselves.
    (p. 98)

6. Among colonial women who lived in seaport towns:
    a. over half of them worked outside their homes as tavernkeepers, domestic servants, laundresses, etc.
    b. even wealthy women planted their own gardens due to a lack of available servants.
    c. widows were not allowed to manage places of business.
    d. midwifery and dressmaking were high-paid occupations.
    (p. 99)

7. African slaves in the Chesapeake region would be more likely than those in the Carolinas to:
    a. work on a larger plantation with more than 20 slaves.
    b. come into daily contact with more whites.
    c. have absentee owners who left white overseers and black drivers to run their plantations.
    d. have been born in Africa.
    (p. 100)

8. The Stono Rebellion of 1739:
    a. was the largest slave revolt of the colonial period.
    b. ignited the last major Indian war in the Chesapeake.
    c. convinced colonial governments to extend political rights to those living in the frontier regions.
    d. was an early sign of tensions between colonists and British troops.
    (pp. 103-104)

9. The First Great Awakening:
    a. reflected a celebration of new rational ideas about religion promoted by the Enlightenment.
    b. led to a more invigorated, stable religious life.
    c. left colonial Americans more divided than ever.
    d. came and went quickly with little lasting impact..
    (pp. 104-107)

10. In the decades before the Seven Years' War, most American colonists could be described as:
    a. proud to be part of the British empire.
    b. indifferent to their place in the British empire.
    c. unhappy with their place in the British empire, but not yet interested in independence.
    d. very unhappy with their place in the British empire and nearly ready to revolt and form a free nation.
    (pp. 108-109)

11. By 1750, royal governors in the British colonies:
    a. were elected by each colony's eligible voters.
    b. had almost dictatorial powers over the colonial assemblies.
    c. had tremendous power in theory, but more limited power in practice.
    d. enjoyed virtually no power, and had to accept whatever colonial assemblies dictated.
    (p. 112)

12. As another war with the French approached in the 1750s, the English politician William Pitt hoped it would result in:
    a. limiting the French control in North America.
    b. total British control over North America.
    c. the colonists abandoning their talk of independence.
    d. a new, independent country emerging.
    (p. 115)

COMPLETION

When the Albany Plan of Union devised by _____ was not approved despite
the danger from new French forts, it illustrated the lack of cohesiveness in colonial
society during the first half of the eighteenth century. The colonies became more
diversified as new _____, both free and enslaved, arrived yearly. Many of
these settled in the _____, where land was more plentiful. Conflicts arose
between the frontier settlers and in the more established communities, including
the uprising of the _____ in Pennsylvania and the _____ movements
in the Carolinas. Meanwhile, other people moved into growing colonial cities, all
of which were _____ thriving on regional and international commerce.
Newly arriving slaves usually went to either the Chesapeake or the _____ of
South Carolina and Georgia. Those who lived on large plantations had relatively
more freedom because they worked on the _____ rather than in labor gangs.
While the ideas of the Enlightenment attracted only the more educated colonists,
many of the others became caught up in the wave of _____ sparked by the
Great Awakening. Preachers such as _____ in Massachusetts and
_____ inflamed religious passions. Other sources of debate included the
benefits and drawbacks of English _____ and _____. On the whole,
however, the American colonists liked being _____.

IDENTIFICATION

You should be able to describe the following key terms, concepts, individuals, and
places and explain their significance:

Terms and Concepts

King William's War

Albany Plan of Union

King George's War

Tenant rebellions

March of the Paxton Boys

South Carolina Regulation

North Carolina Regulation

Great Awakening

Artisans

Battle of Alamance

Journeyman

Apprentice

"Negro election day"

Impressment

Task system

Drivers

Stono Rebellion

Maroon communities

Evangelical Christianity

Enlightenment

Rotten boroughs

Rational Christianity

Balanced constitution

Individuals and Places

George Whitefield   Benjamin Franklin
Fort Necessity   Jonathan Edwards
Ethan Allen and the Green   William Pitt
Mountain Boys

MAP IDENTIFICATION

On the map, label or shade in the following places. In a sentence, note their significance to the chapter. (For reference, consult the maps in *Nation of Nations* on pages 94 and 103).

1. Concentrations of Scotch-Irish settlement in the eighteenth century
2. Concentrations of German settlement in the eighteenth century
3. Concentrations of African-American population (above 50 percent of total population) in the eighteenth century

East Coast

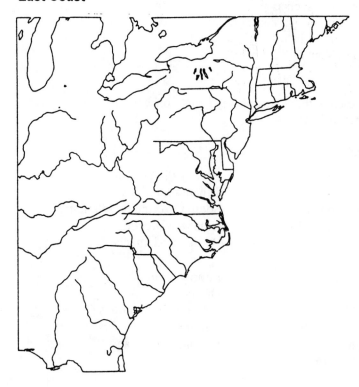

ESSAY

1. Describe the objectives and strategies of the English, the French, and the Indians up to the defeat of the Albany Plan of Union in 1754.

2. What "forces of division" were operating in the British colonies during the first half of the eighteenth century? Discuss with specific reference to at least two of the following areas: immigration, the backcountry, boundary disputes, seaport towns, the strategies of slave resistance, the Great Awakening.

3. Describe the basic outlook of the intellectual movement known as the Enlightenment.

4. Compare and contrast the economy, social structure, and politics of England and America in the eighteenth century.

5. Why was the Great Awakening appealing to colonial society? What groups were least responsive to the revivalist appeals? How and why was the Awakening disruptive both socially and religiously?

6. "To any person in bondage, the condition of slavery must be fundamentally unacceptable, no matter how benevolent a slave's master. Yet the realities of power forced enslaved people every day to confront these inequalities." With this statement in mind, describe your life as a slave in Virginia as of about 1720.

CRITICAL THINKING

EVALUATING EVIDENCE (MAPS AND ILLUSTRATIONS)

1. Based on the map on page 94, in what region of America was there the heaviest concentration of non-English white settlement? What is the significance of that concentration?

2. Based on the map on page 103, in what regions of America was the African-American population growing most rapidly during the eighteenth century? What factors might explain that growth?

3. In "The Old Plantation" (page 101), identify the musical instruments. What might they indicate about the culture of the slave quarters?

PRIMARY SOURCE: George Whitefield Preaches at Middletown, Connecticut[*]

Nathan Cole, a farmer and carpenter residing near Middletown, Connecticut, left the following account of George Whitefield's appearance there in 1740. Cole's narrative conveys the excitement aroused throughout the colonies by Whitefield's preaching.

...I longed to see and hear [Whitefield] and wished he would come this way....And then one morning...there came a messenger and said Mr. Whitfeld...is to preach at Middletown this morning at 10 o clock. I was in my field at work [and] I dropt my tool rotten boroughs rotten boroughs...and run home...and bade my wife to get ready quick to goo and hear Mr. Whitfeld. I brought my hors home and soon mounted and took my wife up and went forward as fast as I thought the hors could bear....We improved every moment to get along as if we was fleeing for our lives, all this while fearing we should be too late to hear the Sarmon, for we had twelve miles to ride double in littel more than an hour.

...I saw before me a Cloud or fog rising—I first thought—off from the great river. But as I came nearer the road I heard a noise, something like a low rumbling thunder, and I presently found it was the rumbling of horses feet coming down the road and this Cloud was a Cloud of dust made by the running of horses feet....And when I came nearer it was like a stedy streem of horses and their riders....Every hors semed to go with all his might to carry his rider to hear the news from heaven for the saving of their Souls. It made me trembel to see the Sight—how the world was in a strugle! I herd no man speak a word all the way...but evry one presing forward in great haste. And when we gat down to the old meating house, thare was a great multitude. It was said to be 3 or 4000 people assembled together....I turned and looked toward the great river and saw the fery boats running swift... bringing over loads of people.... Everything—men, horses and boats—all seamed to be struglin for life. The land and the banks over the river looked black with people and horse all along the 12 miles. I see no man at work in his field, but all seamed to be gone.

When I see Mr. Whitfeld...he looked almost angellical—a young, slim, slender youth before some thousands of people, and with a bold, undaunted countenance. And my hearing how God was with him everywhere as he came along, it solomnized my mind, and put me in a trembling fear before he began to preach, for he looked as if he was Cloathed with authority from the great God...and my hearing him preach

---

[*] From G. L. Walker, *Some Aspects of the Religious Life of New England* (1897).

gave me a heart wound, by god's blessing. My old foundation was broken up and I saw that my righteousness would not save me. Then I was convinced of the doctrine of Election...because all that I could do would not save me, and he [God] had decreed from Eternity who should be saved and who not....

Questions

1. Besides the emotion generated by Whitefield's presence and his preaching, what would have lent such power to his revival meetings? What aspect of this event made the most vivid impression on Nathan Cole, and why?

2. What features stand out in Cole's description of Whitefield? What characteristics of Whitefield drew Cole's particular notice and why? Do these characteristics suggest anything about the source of Whitefield's authority and charisma?

3. When Cole remarked that "I saw that my righteousness would not save me," to what doctrine of the Protestant Reformation was he alluding? When he remarked that "he [God] had decreed from Eternity who should be saved and who not," to what doctrine of the Reformation was he alluding?

TOWARD THE WAR FOR AMERICAN INDEPENDENCE

KEYS TO THE CHAPTER

LEARNING OBJECTIVES

When you have finished studying this chapter, you should be able to:

1. Summarize the outcome of the Seven Years' War and explain the ways in which it affected relations between Britain and its colonies.

2. Describe the evolution of political thought and tactics among Americans who opposed British policies.

3. Explain the significance of the First Continental Congress and the collapse of royal authority in the colonies.

4. Explain the popularity and political importance of *Common Sense*.

THE CHAPTER IN PERSPECTIVE

The disunited colonies finally found a common enemy to unite them. Rivalry for the control of North America climaxed after 1754. The struggle waged among the English, the French, and the Indians had brought on three wars during the first half of the eighteenth century. That struggle culminated in a fourth conflict, the Seven Years' War (1754-1763; known traditionally if misleadingly to Americans as the French and Indian War). But Britain's total victory in that fight and the end of French power in North America did not bring lasting peace. Native Americans struggled to protect their territory and political sovereignty west of the Appalachians. At the same time, Britain's determination to consolidate its American empire revived the ambivalence of many colonials toward the parent country. Parliament hoped to bind the colonies to the British empire with new laws and regulations. This legislation served only to alienate Americans already wary of the inequalities of English society and the corruption of English politics. Popular opposition to Britain's new measures led ultimately to rebellion and independence. With the French enemy out of the way, the British government became the ultimate common enemy that made possible thirteen "united states."

OVERVIEW

Americans liked being English. They celebrated the English triumph over the French. But in the dozen years thereafter, they came to realize that English politicians would not allow them to be English. In short, the Seven Years' War resolved the contest for supremacy in North America but it also set the stage for American independence.

The Seven Years' War was pivotal because it created opposing expectations for the future. Once the French were removed from the frontiers of British America, George III and his ministers could renew their efforts to centralize and consolidate the empire.

The British victory left Americans overflowing with great expectations of the role that they would play in the expanded empire. But many leading Britons charged that Americans had withheld support and even traded with the enemy. Such conflicting perceptions lit the fuse of imperial crisis.

The Imperial Crisis

Britain determined to impose tighter controls on its newly enlarged empire and pay for the expense by raising revenue in the colonies. The new measures of the early 1760s—e.g., the Proclamation of 1763, the Stamp Act, and the Quartering Act—were all designed to advance the cause of centralization.

The timing of these new measures was disastrous. They deflated American expectations of a more equal status and coincided with a downturn in the colonial economy. The new measures abridged what Americans understood to be their constitutional and political liberties.

British actions seemed to confirm American suspicions of a deliberate plot to enslave Americans by depriving them of property and liberty. Americans displayed an unprecedented unity in opposing imperial policy, turning to petitions, crowd actions, and boycotts as resistance tactics. Parliament bowed to pressure from British merchants and repealed the Stamp Act, but reasserted its authority to tax by passing the Townshend Acts in 1767. Americans renewed their resistance, enforcing boycotts with committees of inspection, and affirmed their unity in responses to the Massachusetts Circular Letter. The stationing of British troops erupted into violence with the Boston Massacre.

With the repeal of most of the Townshend duties, American resistance subsided until the Gaspee incident in 1772. The formation of the committees of correspondence fostered intercolonial consensus and spread the scope of the resistance inland. When Britain responded to the Boston Tea Party with the Coercive Acts in 1774, many more Americans joined the cause. The stage was set for concerted intercolonial action.

Toward the Revolution

The growing unity of the resistance movement came to fruition when the First Continental Congress met at Philadelphia in September 1774. Delegates resisted both radical demands for immediate mobilization for war and conservative appeals for accommodation. They denied Parliament any authority in the colonies except the power to regulate trade, but acknowledged the colonies' allegiance to George III.

The collapse of royal authority in Massachusetts was moving the colonies toward a showdown with Britain. As a show of force, General Thomas Gage dispatched troops in April of 1775 to seize arms being stored at Concord. A battle between British soldiers and the Massachusetts militia resulted. In January of 1776, Thomas Paine's *Common Sense* undermined the emotional tie to England by attacking George III, persuading many Americans of the necessity of becoming independent and republican—to become not English, but American.

KEY EVENTS

1756	*Britain and France declare war*
1759	*Wolfe's victory at Quebec:* Britain controls the St. Lawrence
1763	*Treaty of Paris:* ends the Seven Years' War
	Pontiac's Rebellion: Indians strike out in response to white westward migration
	Proclamation of 1763: prohibits settlement west of the Appalachians
1764-65	*Sugar Act and Stamp Act:* Parliament's first attempts to tax colonials directly
	Quartering Act: Parliament orders the colonies to provide housing for British troops
1766	*Repeal of the Stamp Act*
	Declaratory Act: Parliament affirms its authority
1767	*Townshend Duties:* Parliament's third attempt at taxation
	Parliament suspends New York Assembly for refusing to comply with the Quartering Act
1770	*Boston Massacre:* British troops fire on civilians
	Parliament repeals the Townshend Duties except for the tax on tea
1773	*Boston Tea Party*

1774	*Coercive Acts:* Parliament's attempt to punish Massachusetts and undermine the resistance
	First Continental Congress meets at Philadelphia
1775	*Battles of Lexington and Concord*
1776	*Publication of* Common Sense

REVIEW QUESTIONS

MULTIPLE CHOICE

1. The Seven Years' War began in North America with the:
    a. Battle of the Plains of Abraham.
    b. surrender of George Washington at Fort Necessity.
    c. capture of Fort Frontenac by New Englanders.
    d. assault on Philadelphia.
    (p. 121)

2. The Seven Years' War resulted in the:
    a. end of French control over any of North America.
    b. severe limiting of French control in North America.
    c. limiting of French control in North America to New Orleans and the territory west of the Mississippi River.
    d. expansion of French control in North America.
    (p. 123)

3. The Proclamation of 1763:
    a. officially ended the Seven Years' War.
    b. banned colonial trade with any nation other than England.
    c. limited colonial settlement to east of the Appalachian mountains.
    d. declared acts of colonial legislatures null and void.
    (pp. 125-126)

4. Those known as the English "Opposition":
    a. migrated to the colonies to show their unhappiness with King George III.
    b. wanted tougher measures against the colonists in order keep them from even considering independence.
    c. were primarily concerned with the potential abuse of power.
    d. opposed the accession of George III because of his Catholic faith.
    (p. 129)

5. The primary aim of Parliament's passage of the Stamp Act was to:
    a. regulate trade between England and her North American colonies by tightening customs inspection.
    b. remind the colonists that they could be subject to laws to which those back in England were not.
    c. raise revenue for England by placing taxes on legal documents, newspapers, playing cards, etc.
    d. require that all acts of colonial legislatures and local town councils be subject to royal approval.
    (p. 128)

6. Committees of Inspection were established to enforce:
    a. anti-smuggling laws.
    b. the Stamp Act.
    c. the Coercive Acts.
    d. the ban on trade with England.
    (p. 135)

7. Which of the following is TRUE about the outcome of the Stamp Act crisis?
    a. American colonists came to support the idea of virtual representation.
    b. Colonists issued the Declaratory Act announcing their refusal to accept the Stamp Act.
    c. The Stamp Act became more accepted over time, as colonists grew weary of fighting over it.
    d. The Stamp Act was repealed by the British Parliament.
    (pp. 128-132)

8. The Boston Massacre was due principally to the tensions surrounding:
    a. the stationing of British regular troops in the city.
    b. the riots in opposition to the Stamp Act.
    c. British punishment of the city following the Tea Party.
    d. the publication of *Common Sense.*
    (p. 135)

9. The Quebec Act angered American colonists for all of the following reasons EXCEPT:
    a. it seemed tied to the Coercive Acts as another insult.
    b. it provided for a powerful representative assembly in Quebec, which would be left alone by Britain.
    c. it extended the boundaries of Quebec to include all the land between the Ohio and Mississippi Rivers.
    d. it officially recognized the Catholic church in Quebec.
    (p. 139)

10. While representing diverse interests, delegates to the First Continental Congress found a certain similarity they referred to as:
    a. civic virtue.
    b. common sense.
    c. the democratic faith.
    d. Federalism.
    (p. 139)

11. The British marched on Lexington and Concord in 1775 to:
    a. put down an anti-British rebellion in these villages.
    b. arrest French spies believed to be hiding out in the area.
    c. alleviate tensions between British soldiers and American colonists in Boston itself.
    d. seize the arms and ammunition stored by the Provincial Congress.
    (pp. 142-143)

12. In his pamphlet *Common Sense,* Thomas Paine:
    a. appealed directly to King George III to change British policies toward the American colonies.
    b. criticized those who dared talk of independence, but listed numerous reasons why British policies were unjust.
    c. denounced monarchy as a dangerous form of government.
    d. argued that the colonists establish their own independent monarchy in America as their birthright.
    (pp. 143-144)

COMPLETION

For most of the colonial period, Americans liked being _____. By the end of the _____ War, with the British having vanquished the French, American expectations for the future were high. However, the British needed to pay for the _____, and they began tightening control over the colonies in order to maximize profits. Early restrictions included the _____, which prohibited white settlement past the crest of the Appalachian Mountains, and the Sugar Act. Colonial resistance did not really begin, however, until passage of the _____ in 1765. Early resistance focused on the lack of _____ in Parliament and the right of _____, which both the Stamp Act and the Sugar Act removed. The ideological basis for the resistance came from the theories of _____ that property guaranteed liberty, as well as the radical minority in England, called _____. The next wave of resistance began with the passage of the _____, taxes levied in 1767. Leaders such as _____ and _____ whipped up public outrage, which rose even higher after the 1770 confrontation between soldiers and protesters known as the _____. After acts of resistance such as the Tea Party, the British government resolved to punish the colonists, particularly those in Boston, with the _____, which closed the port and tightly restricted the rights of the citizens. In response, colonial leaders called the _____, which denied the right of Parliament to tax or legislate for the colonies. Fighting broke out the next April, beginning with the battles of _____ and _____.

IDENTIFICATION

You should be able to describe the following key terms, concepts, individuals, and places and explain their significance.

Terms and Concepts

Proclamation of 1763	Sugar or Revenue Act
Stamp Act	The "Opposition"
Pontiac's Rebellion	Quartering Act
Virtual representation	Declaratory Act
Townshend Acts	Actual representation
Boston Massacre	Liberty riot
Nonimportation	Gaspee Commission
Tea Act	Boston Tea Party
Coercive Acts	Battle of Lexington and Concord
First Continental Congress	Continental Association
Committees of Correspondence	*Common Sense*
Seven Years' War	Treaty of Paris, 1763

Individuals and Places

James Wolfe	John Locke
George Grenville	Patrick Henry
Sons of Liberty	John Dickinson
George III	Samuel Adams
Thomas Gage	John Adams
Joseph Galloway	Thomas Paine

MAP IDENTIFICATION

On the map, label or shade the following places. In a sentence, note their significance to the chapter. (For reference, consult the map on page 124 of *Nation of Nations*.)

1. Territory claimed by England as of 1763
2. Territory claimed by Spain as of 1763
3. Proclamation Line of 1763
4. Territory claimed by France as of 1763

North America

ESSAY

1. Describe the expectations of Americans and the attitudes of Britons toward Americans after the Seven Years' War. How did those expectations and attitudes set the stage for the crisis that followed?

2. Describe the evolution of American tactics for resisting British policy. Does British policy seem reasonable?

3. Why did many colonists turn from liking being English to seeing themselves as Americans and wanting independence?

4. Was the dispute over taxation and representation a noble appeal to the principles of freedom or merely an issue of the pocketbook? Discuss the motivations of those who led the resistance.

5. Write a letter to the editor of your hometown newspaper, circa 1773, describing your feelings about the developing tensions between the colonists and England. How are you affected by those tensions? What actions would you favor being taken?

CRITICAL THINKING

EVALUATING EVIDENCE (MAPS AND ILLUSTRATIONS)

1. According to the map on page 122, in what period of time and where did the French enjoy their greatest success? At what point did the tide of battle begin to turn in favor of the British?

2. The maps on page 124 indicate the increasing size of the British empire and the diminishing presence of the French. What territory did Britain claim from France by 1763? What was the significance of France's losses in North America for Britain's relations with its colonies?

3. Examine the map on page 127. What geographic feature provided the basis for drawing the Proclamation Line of 1763? Locate the Cumberland Gap. Why was that an important landmark? Locate the British forts in the interior and discuss some of the reasons they were placed where they were.

4. In the porcelain group shown on page 133, "America is represented as a female slave kneeling at the feet of William Pitt." Why was Pitt cast as the liberator of Americans?

PRIMARY SOURCE: Thomas Paine Argues for American Independence*

The following excerpt from *Common Sense* contains some of the modes of reasoning and the rhetorical strategies that made Paine such a successful propagandist for the cause of American independence.

But Britain is the parent country, say some. Then more shame upon her conduct. Even brutes do not devour their young, nor savages make war upon their families; wherefore the assertion, if true, turns to her reproach; but it happens not to be true, or only partly so, and the phrase parent or mother country hath been jesuitically adopted by the—and his parasites, with the low papistical design of gaining an unfair bias on the credulous weakness of our minds. Europe, and not England, is the parent country of America. This new world hath been the asylum for the persecuted lovers of civil and religious liberty from every part of Europe. Hither have they fled, not from the tender embraces of the mother, but from the cruelty of the monster; and it is so far true of England, that the same tyranny which drove the first emigrants from home, pursues their descendants still....Not one-third of the inhabitants, even of this province [Pennsylvania], are of English descent. Wherefore I reprobate the phrase of parent or mother country applied to England only, as being false, selfish, narrow and ungenerous.

* * * * * *

Europe is too thickly planted with kingdoms to be long at peace, and whenever a war breaks out between England and any foreign power, the trade of America goes to ruin because of her connection with Britain. The next war may not turn out like the last, and should it not, the advocates for reconciliation now will be wishing for separation then, because, neutrality in that case, would be a safer convoy than a man of war. Every thing that is right or natural pleads for separation. The blood of the slain, the weeping voice of nature cries, 'TIS TIME TO PART. Even the distance at which the Almighty hath placed England and America is strong natural proof, that the authority of the one, over the other, was never the design of Heaven. The time likewise at which the continent was discovered, adds weight to the argument, and the manner in which it was peopled encreases the force of it. The reformation was preceded by the discovery of America, as if the Almighty graciously meant to open a sanctuary to the persecuted in future years, when home should afford neither friendship nor safety.

---

* From Thomas Paine, *Common Sense* (1776).

Questions

1. When Paine observes that "Even brutes do not devour their young" and "The blood of the slain...cries, 'TIS TIME TO PART," to what events is he alluding?

2. Paine evokes a colonial past in which America figured as an "asylum for the persecuted lovers of civil and religious liberty from every part of Europe." Is his an accurate depiction of early American history? If not, then why does Paine portray the colonial period in those terms?

3. Paine bases his argument for independence on natural law and natural rights rather than on the narrower grounds of "the rights of Englishmen." Underline the passages in the excerpt above where he is making use of arguments from nature. Then explain why, in terms of mobilizing all Americans behind the cause of independence, that strategy was a shrewd one.

4. Why does Paine devote so much attention to arguing that England is not the "parent" country of America? What was he trying to accomplish by criticizing the use of familial metaphors to describe the tie between Britain and the colonies?

THE AMERICAN PEOPLE AND
THE AMERICAN REVOLUTION

KEYS TO THE CHAPTER

LEARNING OBJECTIVES

When you have finished studying this chapter, you should be able to:

1. Explain why the Second Continental Congress adopted the Declaration of Independence and how that document justified revolution.

2. Explain why many Americans became loyalists or tried to remain neutral during the revolutionary struggle.

3. Describe the evolution of military strategy during the war, tracing the course of the conflict from north to south.

4. Explain the significance of the British surrender at Saratoga.

THE CHAPTER IN PERSPECTIVE

It was British attempts to consolidate political control over their American empire that pushed their colonials toward independence. After finally driving France from North America, the British policymakers initiated a decade of crisis and confrontation with their fellow subjects there. Many Americans slowly came to embrace independence as the way to preserve their rights. Misunderstanding and suspicion on both sides gave rise to the American Revolution, a complex conflict that was at once a colonial war of liberation, a civil war among loyal and rebel Americans, and a renewal of the struggle for global supremacy between England and France.

OVERVIEW

Even after the Battle of Bunker Hill, it remained unclear whether most Americans favored independence and would be willing to fight for it.

The Decision for Independence

At the Second Continental Congress in Philadelphia in the spring of 1775, many delegates clung to the hope of a settlement with Britain. Radicals who favored independence moved cautiously. Even as Congress approved the creation of the Continental Army, it declared loyalty to George III. The harsh British response to that overture withered the cause of compromise, opening the way for Congress's adoption of the Declaration of Independence on July 4, 1776.

In the Declaration, Thomas Jefferson set forth a general justification of revolution, denied England any authority in the colonies, and blamed George III for a "long train of abuses and usurpation."

A substantial minority of colonials remained loyal to the king and Parliament. Loyalism was especially strong in those places where violent controversies had raged during the decades before 1776. They feared that the break from Britain would plunge America into anarchy or civil war.

The Fighting in the North

The British planned a conventional war. The British army was a seasoned professional fighting force, while the Continentals, under George Washington, lacked both numbers and military discipline. Washington had to design a defensive, hit-and-run strategy to offset the weakness of his force.

In 1776 the British evacuated Boston, took New York City, and drove the Continentals into a retreat through New York and New Jersey. But as winter set in, Washington recouped some credibility at the Battles of Trenton and Princeton. Many civilians, alienated by the British army's harsh treatment, switched to the rebel cause. In the summer campaign of 1777, the British took Philadelphia but suffered a disastrous defeat at Saratoga, New York.

The Turning Point

The victory at Saratoga marked a turning point. Soon thereafter, France and Spain allied with American rebels. The war spread to Europe, forcing the British to disperse their army to fend off challenges all over the world.

So British forces pulled back from Philadelphia to New York City. The previous winter had been a harrowing one for the Continentals at Valley Forge, Pennsylvania. Though they broke camp with newly instilled training and discipline, the morale of Washington's Continentals began to fray, occasionally leading to mutinies. The Continental rank-and-file had been drawn from propertyless and desperate Americans; Congress found it easy to neglect them.

The Struggle in the South

The British now turned to a southern strategy, expecting support from those loyal to the crown. Though loyalists were numerous in the Georgia and Carolina backcountry, they met determined resistance from rebel irregulars.

Nathanael Greene, in command of the Continental Army in the South, proved an ingenious strategist. His support for the rebel partisans and his careful treatment of a civilian population disenchanted by Lord Cornwallis's marauding army frustrated British efforts to take the Carolinas. The British, fearful of estranging whites, had chosen not to mobilize one large group of southerners who might have fought with them to win liberty—African-American slaves. Instead, blacks were recruited, reluctantly, for the Continental Army.

The World Turned Upside Down

Cornwallis made an unsuccessful bid for victory at Yorktown, Virginia, in 1781. With the tide of war in Europe turning against them as well, the British decided to cut their losses in America and agreed to the Treaty of Paris in 1783. The pact granted not only independence but a generous boundary settlement as well.

KEY EVENTS

1775	*Second Continental Congress Creates Continental Army*
	Battle of Bunker Hill
1776	*British troops evacuate Boston but occupy New York City*
	Declaration of Independence
	Battle of Trenton: Washington counterattacks
1777	*British summer drive to occupy Philadelphia*
	Battles of Brandywine Creek, Germantown: Continentals are defeated twice
	Battle of Saratoga: a major rebel victory
	Continental Army encamps for winter at Valley Forge
1778	*France allies with Americans*
	British shift focus to the South: Savannah falls

1780	*British occupy Charleston*
	Battle of King's Mountain, South Carolina: rebel victory
1781	*Cornwallis surrenders at Yorktown*
1783	*Treaty of Paris:* Britain recognizes the United States as an independent nation

REVIEW QUESTIONS

MULTIPLE CHOICE

1. The Battle of Bunker Hill showed that:
>   a. the colonists still lacked the essential will to fight.
>   b. the Americans were almost certain to win their independence.
>   c. the British had underestimated General Washington's military skills.
>   d. American colonists would fight and die in their dispute with the British.
>   *(pp. 147-148)*

2. In the Declaration of Independence:
>   a. King George III is blamed for a long list of abuses against the colonies.
>   b. Parliament is blamed for the breakdown of relations with the colonies.
>   c. the colonists still held out an "Olive Branch Petition" to King George III.
>   d. George Washington was named as acting President.
>   *(p. 149)*

3. In the Carolinas, Loyalists were most numerous among the:
>   a. ordinary folk living in the backcountry.
>   b. propertyless day laborers in the port cities.
>   c. wealthiest planters in the coastal regions.
>   d. members of Anglican congregations.
>   *(p. 151)*

4. Hessian soldiers participated in the American Revolution:
>   a. as voluntary supporters of the British cause.
>   b. as paid mercenaries for the British.
>   c. as voluntary supporters of the American cause.
>   d. as paid mercenaries for the Americans.
>   *(p. 153)*

5. "Women of the Army" were:
   a. women who dressed up as men in order to fight.
   b. wives of the Continental Army soldiers who fought on the home front by tending farms, mills, shops, etc.
   c. relatively poor women who followed the Continental Army, performing chores such as cooking and nursing.
   d. wealthy women who nursed wounded soldiers.
   (pp. 153-154)

6. The Continentals who crossed the Delaware on Christmas night, 1776 were:
   a. evacuating Philadelphia as it was being overrun by the British forces.
   b. deserting the army because of miserable conditions.
   c. ambushed by the British and hanged for treason.
   d. led by George Washington and en route to a successful surprise attack.
   (p. 156)

7. The French decided to actively support the Americans against the British:
   a. because of their admiration for the ideals expressed in the Declaration of Independence.
   b. after the surrender of British forces at Saratoga convinced the French the Continentals could win.
   c. after the fall of New York to the British convinced the French the Continentals were on the verge of defeat.
   d. as soon as the Seven Years' War came to an end.
   (p. 158)

8. The last major phase in the fighting of the American Revolutionary War took place in:
   a. Canada.
   b. New England.
   c. the Middle States.
   d. the South.
   (pp. 162, 168)

9. During the American Revolution, African-American slaves:
   a. were unwilling to fight for either the British or the Continentals.
   b. fought for the British when promised their freedom, but not for the Continentals, whom they distrusted.
   c. fought only for the Continentals.
   d. were willing to fight for whichever side promised them freedom.
   (p. 167)

10. Benedict Arnold defected to the British cause:
    a. when he became convinced the Continentals could not win.
    b. because he despised the French.
    c. due to his personal debt and his feeling that the Continental Congress had not treated the Continental Army fairly.
    d. when George Washington became Commander-in-Chief.
    (p. 168)

11. Which of the following is TRUE about the British surrender at Yorktown?
    a. The British decided after Yorktown to redouble their efforts to put down the American Revolution.
    b. It proved that the colonials were the decisive factors in winning independence, not the largely symbolic French effort.
    c. It might not have been necessary had the British navy arrived in time.
    d. It proved the effectiveness of guerrilla warfare.
    (pp. 168-169)

COMPLETION

The question General Gage asked before the _____ was "will they fight?" The subsequent years proved that the answer was yes. After the British government rejected the _____ and British attacks withered the cause of reconciliation, Congress gave Thomas Jefferson the job of drafting the _____, which blamed _____ for the abuses that led to American independence. However, a strong contingent of _____ existed in the colonies. Moreover, the Continental Army was undermanned and relied heavily on the support of _____, who fought when the British army came close to their neighborhoods. The British gained the early military advantage, occupying _____ and _____. The turning point occurred at _____, the American victory that convinced _____ to enter the war on the American side. The British subsequently turned their attention to the _____, which they believed held the more valuable colonies. They hoped to stir up support in the backcountry, but militia leaders such as Frances Marion and _____, also known as "the Gamecock," convinced the settlers in the region that only the rebels could maintain order. British leaders also hoped to stir up the _____ of the region, but desperation eventually caused Americans to enlist blacks willing to fight for the revolutionary cause. The war finally ended at _____, where Cornwallis surrendered to Washington.

IDENTIFICATION

You should be able to describe the following key terms, concepts, individuals, and places and explain their significance.

Terms and Concepts

Battle of Bunker Hill	Battle of Yorktown
Loyalists	Homespun
Continental Army	Hessians
Battle of Germantown	Partisan war in the South
Battle of King's Mountain	Treaty of Paris, 1783
Second Continental Congress	Declaration of Independence
Standing army	Militia
Battle of Princeton	Battle of Saratoga
Siege of Charleston	Battle of Camden

Individuals and Places

William Howe	Thomas Jefferson
Charles, Lord Cornwallis	John Burgoyne
George Washington	Horatio Gates
Benedict Arnold	Henry Clinton
Valley Forge	Baron von Steuben
Thayendanegea	Nathanael Greene
Francis Marion	Comte de Rochambeau

MAP IDENTIFICATION

On the map on the following page, label or shade in the following places. In a sentence, note their significance to the chapter. (For reference, consult the map on page 165 of *Nation of Nations*.)

1. site of the siege of Charleston
2. site of the battle of Camden
3. site of the battle of King's Mountain
4. site of the battle of Guilford Courthouse
5. site of Yorktown

South Carolina

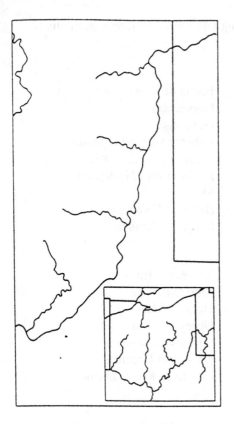

ESSAY

1. List and explain several ways the Declaration of Independence justified the colonies' break with Great Britain.

2. How did the Revolution affect the lives of non-combatants—men and women, slave and free?

3. The answer to the question "would they fight," the text says, was "yes—but on their own terms." Explain who did or didn't fight—and why.

4. What was the most important reason that the British lost the War for Independence? Defend your response.

CRITICAL THINKING

EVALUATING EVIDENCE (MAPS AND ILLUSTRATIONS)

1. Judging from the map of the southern campaigns on page 165, where were civilians exposed to the greatest dangers?

2. What does the picture of the Continental soldiers on page 160 suggest about the grievances of Washington's army? What were the sources and consequences of disaffection within the ranks of the Continentals?

3. Heroic paintings (such as John Trumbull's depiction of the presentation of the Declaration on page 150) often were designed to teach certain lessons or celebrate certain virtues rather then just representing a historical event. What might Trumbull be trying to say to citizens of a brand-new republic?

PRIMARY SOURCE: Civilians and Soldiers in the War for Independence*

Sally Wister was 15 years old at the time that she made these entries in a diary, writing them as if she addressed Deborah Norris. The Wisters, a Quaker family, also lived in Philadelphia, but moved to the countryside when it appeared that the British would occupy that city.

> *September, 1777: Yesterday... two Virginia officers called at our house, and informed us that the British army had crossed the Schuykill [River]...and that General Washington and army were near Pottsgrove. Well, thee may be sure we were sufficiently scared; however, the road was very still till evening. About seven o'clock we heard a great noise. To the door we all went. A large number of waggons, with about three hundred of the Philadelphia militia. They begged for drink, and several pushed into the house. One of those that entered was a little tipsy, and had a mind to be saucy. I then thought it time for me to retreat; so figure me (mightily scared, as not having presence of mind enough to face so many of the military) running in at one door, and out at another, all in a shake with fear; but after a little, seeing the officers appear gentlemanly and the soldier civil, I called reason to my aid....They did not offer to take their quarters with us; so, with many blessings, and as many adieus, they marched off....*

> *September 26th: We were unusually silent all the morning....About twelve o'clock, cousin Jesse heard that General Howe's army had*

---

* From *Sally Wister's Journal: A True Narrative* (1902).

moved down towards Philadelphia. Then, my dear, our hopes and fears were engaged for you....I was standing in the kitchen....when somebody came to me in a hurry, screaming, "Sally, Sally, here are the light horse!" This was by far the greatest fright I had endured....They rode up to the door and halted, and enquired if we had horses to sell; he answered negatively. "Have not you, sir," to my father, "two black horses?"—"Yes, but have no mind to dispose of them." My terror had by this time nearly subsided. The officer and men behaved perfectly civil...the men, to our great joy, were Americans....

October 19th: Two genteel men of the military order rode up to the door: "Your servant, ladies," etc.; ask'd if they could have quarters for General Smallwood. Aunt F. thought she could accommodate them as well as most of her neighbors,—said they could. One of the officers dismounted, and wrote "Smallwood's Quarters" over the door, which secured us from straggling soldiers....Dr. Gould usher'd the men into our parlour and introduc'd them,—"General Smallwood, Captain Furnival, Major Stodard, Mr. Prig, Captain Finley, and Mr. Clagan, Colonel Wood, and Colonel Line. These last two did not come with the General. They are Virginians....The General and suite, are Marylanders....How new is our situation! I feel in good spirits, though surrounded by an army, the house full of officers, the yard alive with soldiers—very peaceable sort of people, tho'. They eat like other folks, talk like them, and behave themselves with elegance; so I will not be afraid of them, that I won't.

Questions

1. Why was Sally Wister so apprehensive and fearful in the presence of soldiers? What earlier events in the war might she have known about that prompted her concern?

2. Does the passage indicate any differences between the behavior of the militia and that of Continental Army officers?

3. Once she overcame her fear, what was Sally Wister's attitude toward the militia and the Continental Army? When she remarked, "How new is our situation!" to what might she have been referring other than the presence of the military?

4. Was the attitude toward and treatment of the army described here typical of relations between American civilians and American soldiers during the War for Independence?

5. What was happening in Philadelphia at the time that Sally Wister wrote her diary entries?

CRISIS AND CONSTITUTION

KEYS TO THE CHAPTER

LEARNING OBJECTIVES

When you have finished studying this chapter, you should be able to:

1. Define republicanism and explain how the first state constitutions reflected the postwar view of republicanism.

2. Describe the Articles of Confederation and explain why it proved unsatisfactory.

3. Explain the ways in which the settlement of the West gave rise to both diplomatic and domestic political conflict, yet produced the Northwest Ordinance, which reconfigured sectional tension.

4. Explain how American revolutionaries understood "equality" and how this view shaped the scope and limits of social changes during the postrevolutionary period.

5. Describe the framing of the federal Constitution and explain why many Americans were willing to establish a strong national government.

THE CHAPTER IN PERSPECTIVE

American rebels had won their independence from Great Britain. In many ways the war heightened existing divisions within American society. Added to older tensions over racial, ethnic, sectional, and religious diversity were a new set of difficulties arising from independent nationhood and the challenge of crafting a workable republican government. At the core of the crisis was the challenge to balance state against central and (within those) legislative against executive power. The first instinct, a natural consequence of their rebellion against King George, was to vest power in the state legislatures. But that initial strategy proved unworkable.

OVERVIEW

The Revolution did not create a national identity. Most inhabitants of "these United States" were less committed to creating a single national republic than to organizing thirteen separate and loosely federated *state* republics. A sense of crisis grew as various political entities and social groups began to fragment.

Republican Experiments

The conviction that republics were not suited to large territories influenced the drafting of state constitutions. These crucial early experiments in establishing republican government maintained the basic structure of the old colonial governments, but altered dramatically the balance of power among the branches of government. Popularly elected legislatures became the dominant force in the government. Revolutionaries thus rejected British mixed government in favor of separation of powers. They also insisted their state constitutions be written down, a specified code separate from and superior to the government.

Eagerly writing state constitutions, Amricans largely ignored national government. Not until 1781 did all the states approve the Articles of Confederation. These provided essentially for a continuation of the Second Continental Congress but left the crucial powers entirely to the states. Few leaders even perceived a need to define how power between the states and the national government should be distributed.

The Temptations of Peace

Domestic turmoil and foreign threats forced American leaders to rethink this question of national versus state power. As the British tried to lure Vermonters into Canada and the Spanish encouraged secession among southwesterners, some states squabbled over conflicting claims to western land.

The settlement of the West also triggered controversy by democratizing state legislatures. Fears of democratic excess shaped the landmark Northwest Ordinance of 1787, which withheld full self-government from these new territories until statehood. Even so, the Ordinance established an orderly way of incorporating the frontier into the federal system and outlawed slavery there.

Northern laws abolishing slavery and an increase in manumissions in the upper South, swelled the growth of the free black community and altered its character. However, slavery continued to expand along with the cotton economy. Contests over the west were aggravated by battles over monetary policy. National and state governments proved as powerless to redress postwar economic disruption as they had in coping with problems posed by the frontier.

Republican Society

As political leaders struggled to shape new republican governments, ordinary Americans sought to create a new republican society based on the ideal of equality. Craft workers and laborers sought more respect. Women won better educational opportunities. States with official churches gradually "disestablished" them. Yet revolutionaries stopped short of extending equality to blacks and women. Their view of equality emphasized leveling the top by abolishing aristocratic privilege rather than raising up the lowest social groups.

From Confederation to Constitution

In the mid-1780s the political crisis of the Confederation came to a head, prompted by the controversy over a proposed treaty with Spain and a farmers' rebellion in Massachusetts. The response was the Constitutional Convention of 1787. Instead of revising the Articles of Confederation, it produced an entirely new frame of government the Federal Constitution.

The Constitution provided for separation of powers among a two-house national legislature, a strong executive, and a judiciary. A deadlock among the delegates over the issue of representation was broken by a compromise which provided for equal representation of states in the upper house of Congress and representation proportional to population in the lower house.

Opponents of the Constitution, the Anti-Federalists, feared that a strong central government would become corrupt and arbitrary. Federalists promised to add a bill of rights to the Constitution after ratification. In accepting the Constitution, the states repudiated their earlier commitment to legislative supremacy, revised their former insistence upon state sovereignty, rejected the improbability of a national republic, and admitted that most people's behavior reflected interest rather than virtue.

KEY EVENTS

1781	*Articles of Confederation ratified*
1784	*Spain closes the Mississippi River:* hoped to lure Americans living in the Old Southwest into the Spanish empire
1785	*Jay-Gardoqui Treaty negotiated but not ratified:* sectional tensions enflamed by the treaty's provisions
1786	*Shays' Rebellion:* farmers rise in armed protest
	Annapolis convention: calls for revising the Articles
1787	*Congress adopts the Northwest Ordinance*
	Constitutional Convention: delegates draft an entirely new framework for the national government
1787-1788	*Publication of the* Federalist Papers
1791	*Bill of Rights adopted*

REVIEW QUESTIONS

MULTIPLE CHOICE

1. The new state constitutions set up during the American Revolution:
    a. showed a distrust for the "civic virtue" of citizens.
    b. gave each state's governor veto power over legislation, and the opportunity for wide patronage in making office appointments.
    c. granted universal suffrage to all adult males, removing all property requirements.
    d. called for annual elections of the legislature.
    (pp. 173-175)

2. The Articles of Confederation set up a national government in the United States that could best be described as:
    a. unofficial.
    b. monarchical.
    c. weak.
    d. powerful.
    (pp. 175-176)

3. Maryland refused to ratify the Articles of Confederation:
    a. until a clause protecting religious freedom was specifically added.
    b. until all states had given up their claims to lands in the West.
    c. unless the nation's capital was moved to Washington, D.C.
    d. out of fear that it granted the new national government too much power.
    (pp. 179-180)

4. The Northwest Ordinance provided all of the following EXCEPT:
    a. honoring the rights of Indian tribes.
    b. outlawing slavery in the Northwest Territory.
    c. new states admitted to the union as equal partners of the original states.
    d. support for public education.
    (pp. 182-183)

5. In the decades immediately after the American Revolution:
    a. the Confederation Congress outlawed slavery in all the Northern states.
    b. the importation of African slaves was outlawed.
    c. Northern states began to abolish slavery.
    d. Upper South states such as Virginia and Maryland made it more difficult for owners to free their slaves.
    (pp. 183-185)

6. In the years right after the American Revolution:
    a. postwar inflation was ended by regulation of the economy.
    b. merchants and creditors in most states favored the printing of more paper money to stimulate economic demand.
    c. state legislatures became battlegrounds of competing economic factions.
    d. a relatively stable economy prevailed.
    (pp. 185-186)

7. Beyond winning independence, perhaps the most significant change brought about by the American Revolution was the:
    a. dramatic redistribution of wealth.
    b. growing power of democratic ideas.
    c. election of women to major political offices.
    d. the growing acceptance of an aristocratic elite.
    (pp. 186-191)

8. "Republican motherhood" referred to:
    a. the role of women in the home to raise their children as informed and self-reliant citizens.
    b. a growing number of women elected to public office.
    c. the equality of women in parenting and in a marriage.
    d. leaders in the movement to grant women the right to vote.
    (pp. 189-190)

9. Shays' Rebellion demonstrated that:
    a. disagreements between states were becoming more violent.
    b. the government was failing to protect property rights.
    c. revolts by unemployed laborers in seaport cities were threatening to destroy the United States from within.
    d. the U.S. Constitution could not prevent Americans from resorting to violence to achieve their ends.
    (p. 192)

10. Which of the following was NOT part of James Madison's "Virginia Plan"?
    a. a more powerful central government.
    b. a bicameral Congress with representation based on a state's population for the lower house, and two votes per state in the Senate.
    c. an executive who would be chosen by Congress.
    d. an independent federal judiciary as the third branch of government.
    (p. 194)

11. Anti-Federalists:
    a. published "The Federalist Papers" to expose the class bias of those who had written the U.S. Constitution.
    b. warned that the central government proposed under the new Constitution would be weak and ineffective.
    c. criticized the framers of the Constitution for failing to include a national bill of rights.
    d. opposed the ratification of the Constitution because of its silence on the issue of slavery.
    (p. 196)

12. In his famous tenth essay in "The Federalist Papers," James Madison:
    a. defended the Constitution's acceptance of slavery, arguing that the "peculiar institution" would eventually die out.
    b. criticized the very Constitution he had helped to create.
    c. explained that the vast size of the U.S. would actually make it more likely to sustain a republic since no one faction could dominate.
    d. outlined the debate over ratifying the Constitution for historical reference, but refused to take sides personally.
    (p. 196)

COMPLETION

Most of the revolutionary generation identified more with their _____ than with the _____. Accordingly, the first American _____ were created in the states. These documents feared the spread of _____, after their experiences with George III. This fear carried over into the document that created the new federal government, the _____. However, the subsequent decade revealed that this new government was inadequate. Among the problems it proved unable to solve were the distribution of _____ lands, which was largely solved by the _____. The war had transformed not only American ideas about government but also the nation's society and _____. The republican ideal of an "aristocracy of _____" encouraged the rise of entrepreneurs and a new generation of politicians. Meanwhile, the rights of women became a social issue after the publication of _____ book, *Vindication of the Rights of Women.* Americans such as _____ and Judith Sargent Murray promoted the idea of _____ so that women would be capable of raising the virtuous citizenry the nation needed. Yet even as these debates were arising, a change was occurring in American political principles during the efforts to ratify the _____. Alexander Hamilton and _____, the primary authors of the _____, argued that the government should be based on balancing the _____ of men rather than relying on their _____. They believed a strong federal government would limit the dangers of _____. Their new vision of government triumphed over that of the _____, who wanted to keep primary authority in the _____, but only after a bitter debate.

IDENTIFICATION

You should be able to describe the following key terms, concepts, individuals, and places and explain their significance.

Terms and Concepts

New state constitutions
Articles of Confederation
Northwest Ordinance of 1787
"The peculiar institution"
The Federalist Papers
Society of Cincinnati
Shays' Rebellion
Annapolis Convention
Virginia Plan
Bill of Rights
Written and unwritten constitutions

Bicameral legislature
Landed and landless states
Manumission
Republican motherhood
Disestablishment
Jay-Gardoqui Treaty
Constitutional Convention
New Jersey Plan
Antifederalism
Land speculation

Individuals and Places

David Hume
James Madison
Alexander Hamilton
John Jay

Cumberland Gap
Patrick Henry
Benjamin Rush
Judith Sargent Murray

MAP IDENTIFICATION

On the map on the following page, label or shade in the following places. In a sentence, note their significance to the chapter. (For reference, consult the map on page 179 of *Nation of Nations*.)

1. British Canada
2. Spanish Louisiana
3. Territory ceded by Virginia in 1784 and 1792
4. Territory ceded by Connecticut in 1782

Present day East and Midwest

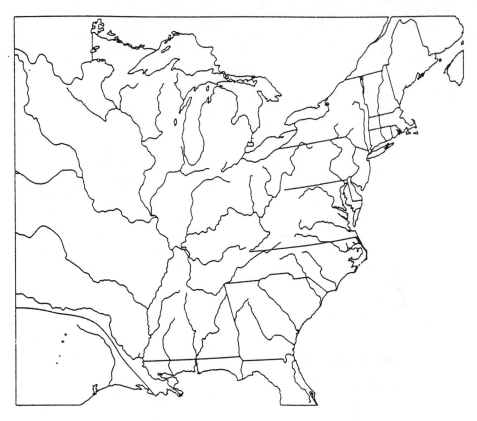

ESSAY

1. Describe the weaknesses of the Articles of Confederation. Why did Americans create a weak national government?

2. How did the Jay-Gardoqui Treaty and Shays' Rebellion contribute to the convening of the Constitutional Convention?

3. Compare the New Jersey and the Virginia plans at the Constitutional Convention. What caused each state to favor the plan it proposed?

4. What concepts of equality directed the actions of the revolutionaries?

5. Did the Constitution advance or set back the principles of the Revolution? Defend your answer in a letter to a friend in England by showing clearly the changes in political philosophy that the Constitution demonstrated.

6. Were the early republican ideals realistic or idealistic? Do you think selfless virtue or selfish interest is the soundest base upon which to build a government? Why?

CRITICAL THINKING

EVALUATING EVIDENCE (MAPS AND ILLUSTRATIONS)

1. Discuss the ways in which the map of western land claimed by the states on page 179 helps to explain the intensity of the conflict between landed and landless states and the way in which that conflict was finally resolved.

2. The picture of a New York crowd pulling down a statue of George III (see page 174) illustrates the mistrust of the executive branch among the revolutionary generation. What events during the Confederation period encouraged Americans to adopt a federal constitution with a strong executive?

3. The picture of a black Methodist congregation in Philadelphia on page 184 reflects the increasing appeal of evangelical Christianity to African-Americans. What features of the evangelical message might have attracted black Americans?

PRIMARY SOURCE: The Constitutional Convention Debates the Slave Trade[*]

Article I, Section 9 of the federal Constitution prohibited Congress from outlawing the slave trade before 1808. That provision replaced an earlier draft that forbade any restraint of the "importation of persons" by the national legislature. That initial clause prompted a debate among delegates Roger Sherman of Connecticut, George Mason and Edmund Randolph of Virginia, and John Rutledge and Charles Pinckney of South Carolina. What follows are notes of that debate as recorded by James Madison.

> [Roger Sherman] was for leaving the clause as it stands. He disapproved of the slave trade; yet as the States were now possessed of the right to import slaves as the public good did not require it to be taken away from them, & as it was expedient to have as few objections as possible to the proposed scheme of Government, he thought it best to leave the matter as we find it. He observed that the abolition of Slavery seemed to be going on in the U.S. & that the good sense of the several States would probably by degrees complete it....

---

[*] From *Records of the Federal Convention,* August 22, 1787.

Col. Mason. This infernal traffic originated in the avarice of British merchants. The British Government constantly checked the attempts of Virginia to put a stop to it. The present question concerns not the importing States alone but the whole Union. The evil of having slaves was experienced during the late war. Had slaves been treated as they might have been by the Enemy, they would have proved dangerous instruments in their hand. But their folly dealt by the slaves, as it did by the Tories. He mentioned the dangerous insurrections of the slaves in Greece and Sicily.... Maryland & Virginia he said had already prohibited the importation of slaves expressly. North Carolina had done the same in substance. All this would be in vain if South Carolina and Georgia be at liberty to import. The Western people are already calling out for slaves for their new lands, and will fill that Country with slaves if they can be got through South Carolina and Georgia. Slavery discourages arts & manufactures. The poor despise labor when performed by slaves. They prevent the immigration of Whites, who really enrich & Strengthen a Country. They produce the most pernicious effect on manners. Every master of slaves is born a petty tyrant. They bring the judgment of heaven on a Country.... By an inevitable chain of causes & effects providence punishes national sins, by national calamities. He lamented that some of our Eastern brethren had from a lust of gain embarked in this nefarious traffic. As to the States being in possession of the Right to import, this was the case with many other rights, now to be properly given up. He held it essential in every point of view that the General Government should have power to prevent the increase in slavery.

Mr. Pinckney. If slavery be wrong, it is justified by the example of all the world. He cited the case of Greece, Rome & other ancient States; the sanction given by France, England, Holland & other modern States. In all ages one-half of mankind have been slaves. If the Southern States were let alone they will probably of themselves stop importations....An attempt to take away the right as proposed will produce serious objections to the Constitution which he wished to see adopted....

Mr. Rutlidge. If the Convention thinks that North Carolina, South Carolina & Georgia will ever agree to the plan, unless their right to import slaves be untouched, the expectation is vain. The people of those States will never be such fools as to give up so important an interest....

Mr. Randolph was for committing in order that some middle ground might, if possible, be found. He could never agree to the clause as it stands. He would sooner risk the constitution. He dwelt on the dilemma to which the Convention was exposed. By agreeing to the clause, it would revolt the Quakers, the Methodists, and many others in the States having no slaves. On the other hand, two States might be lost to the Union....

Questions

1. On what grounds did Roger Sherman defend the clause that barred Congress from restraining the slave trade? In what ways did the opposition of the South Carolinians bear out Sherman's position?

2. What were George Mason's objections to the slave trade? What do his objections indicate about his view of African-Americans?

3. What did Edmund Randolph see as "the dilemma to which the Convention was exposed"?

4. How do you account for the fact that two southerners, Mason and Randolph, lodged the strongest objections to the clause which might have continued the slave trade indefinitely?

5. Why did South Carolinians finally accept the compromise on the slave trade embodied in Article I, Section 9 of the federal Constitution?

THE REPUBLIC LAUNCHED

KEYS TO THE CHAPTER

LEARNING OBJECTIVES

When you have finished studying this chapter, you should be able to:

1. Discuss the differences between the subsistence and commercial economies in the United States in 1789.

2. Describe Alexander Hamilton's financial program and the reasons it provoked opposition.

3. Trace the highlights of American relations with Spain, Britain, and France through this decade.

4. Describe the origins of the Federalist and Republican parties in the 1790s, their principles, and their main sources of support.

5. Explain the relationship between the party system and social and economic divisions in the nation.

6. Explain the significance of the 1800 presidential election.

THE CHAPTER IN PERSPECTIVE

The Constitution was intended to correct the flaws of the Articles of Confederation by strengthening the national government. Yet most Americans retained a strong suspicion of government power. Thus, launching the new government was filled with peril. The Revolution had strengthened the ideology of republicanism, but Americans with different political, social, and economic visions of the Republic's future interpreted republicanism differently. More particularly, an emerging market economy began both to rally one segment of Americans and to alienate another— foreshadowing the continuing link of economic growth to social condition and political opinion. This conflict, which was central to the struggle over ratification of the Constitution, intensified after 1789. And, when war resumed between Britain and France in this period, the United States found its rights and independence challenged. In sum, the first years under the Constitution represented a further working out of domestic and international problems that harked back to the Revolution and its meaning for the American people.

OVERVIEW

The political and social controversy that erupted over a new excise tax on whiskey frames a more fundamental question in the tumultuous 1790s, the first decade of the Republic's existence under the new Constitution. Could the new government unite a socially diverse nation? The "Whiskey Rebellion" thus illustrates a central purpose of the chapter: to describe the basic division in the United States between commercial and semi-subsistence economies, and how this division was central to the development of two competing political parties.

1789: A Social Portrait

As the new government began operation in 1789, the Republic could be said to be divided roughly between commercial and semi-subsistence areas of the country. Hector St. John de Crèvecoeur celebrated the equality that marked semi-subsistence farm families, where wealth was fairly evenly distributed and where people tried to provide as much of their own food and wants as they could. Limited in contacts beyond their local community, they seldom saw cash, functioning in a largely barter economy. Benjamin Franklin, by contrast, symbolized the world of commerce. In his writings, he praised the marketplace and upheld the commercial side of America; he exemplified how urban economies and commercial farm families were tied to larger markets, where specialized goods or services were sold and the social distance between the rich and the poor was more striking.

Americans who participated in the commercial economy held attitudes about wealth and power that were different from those who lived in semi-subsistence areas. Urban merchants and workers as well as commercial farmers had generally supported the Constitution during the debate over ratification, while semi-subsistence farmers had tended to oppose it, fearing too much concentration of power in the hands of aristocrats and urban merchants. Content with their lives and harboring the traditional fear of taxes, debt, and intrusive government, they wanted to preserve their society as it was.

The New Government

Reassuring the more fearful was the prestige of George Washington, who more than any individual personified the Republic. Washington organized the executive branch into departments and created a cabinet of advisors. The most important positions in the cabinet went to Alexander Hamilton, as secretary of the treasury, and Thomas Jefferson, as secretary of state. To mollify opponents of the Constitution, Congress approved and the states ratified a series of amendments to safeguard certain basic liberties. These first ten amendments became known as the Bill of Rights.

A strong nationalist, Hamilton emerged as the cabinet's dominant figure. He worked to strengthen the power of the federal government by assuming the states' remaining Revolutionary war debts and funding, or paying, the outstanding federal debt. Congress finally approved these policies along with the decision to locate the permanent capital on the Potomac River. Eager to tie the wealthy to the new government, Hamilton also proposed that Congress charter a national bank to aid the Treasury in its transactions, a protective tariff to stimulate manufacturing, and a series of internal or excise taxes (the one on whiskey was most controversial). Congress eventually approved most of Hamilton's recommendations. His argument that the Constitution gave the national government implied as well as explicit powers and that the document had to be interpreted loosely persuaded Washington to accept the national bank.

While these ideas appealed especially to citizens active in the commercial life of the nation and in fact produced prosperity, they stimulated fears among other Americans. Eventually the Republican party, organized by James Madison and headed by Thomas Jefferson, opposed the policies of Hamilton's supporters, who retained the Federalist label. Drawing support from the semi-subsistence sector, Republicans still harbored Revolutionary era fears that a corrupt aristocracy would come to dominate American society—that financial speculators, wealthy bankers, and unprincipled politicians would gain power. They endorsed a strict construction of the Constitution, and wanted a less active federal government.

Expansion and Turmoil in the West

Another way to demonstrate the effectiveness of the new government was to strengthen control of the West. Washington dispatched an army that defeated an Indian confederacy, opening new tracts of land in the Ohio Valley to white settlement. Thomas Pinckney negotiated a favorable treaty with Spain that allowed western farmers to use the Mississippi River to ship their produce. Washington also felt compelled to send an army against the citizens in western Pennsylvania who were agitating against Hamilton's excise tax. But the government had overreacted, for the army encountered little resistance and easily restored order.

The Emergence of Political Parties

The ideology of republicanism taught Americans to fear parties. Yet social conditions, which required a mechanism by which diverse groups could voice their views, encouraged parties. Still, it took the sharp controversy over Hamilton's domestic policies to initiate the formation of the first national parties in American history.

Differences over foreign policy were also crucial to the formation of parties. The French Revolution became the focus of controversy in the United States. When monarchical England and revolutionary France went to war, Washington pursued a neutral course. Hamiltonians, however, favored Britain, while the Jeffersonians backed France. Then when efforts to settle the differences between the United States and Britain failed, Jay's Treaty (1795), which tied the nation economically to Britain, provoked bitter debate and further stimulated the creation of rival parties.

Federalists believed in order and hierarchy and supported a loose construction of the Constitution (to allow the federal government to actively encourage commerce and manufacturing). The Republican party of Madison and Jefferson, fearing monarchy and aristocracy, opposed the Federalists. The split reflected the divide between commercial and semi-subsistence America.

In 1796 Washington, wearied by the partisan battles, announced that he would not seek a third term. In America's first contested presidential election, John Adams, the Federalist candidate, defeated Jefferson, who in an odd turn of events was elected vice president. Federalists would hold on to an ordered world a while longer, even as they promoted a more modern economy; Republicans, tied to another suspicion of power, nevertheless would herald future trends toward increasing personal liberty and democracy.

The Presidency of John Adams

Preoccupations with America's role in European affairs continued during the administration of John Adams. France demanded a bribe to stop violating American neutral rights. Adams responded by fighting a naval "Quasi-War." Meanwhile, Federalist-sponsored restrictive legislation—the Alien and Sedition Acts—provoked a Republican assertion that states could block national laws.

Though Adams concluded a satisfactory peace with France, Federalist support eroded due to their opposition to civil liberties and an increasingly fierce personal feud between Adams and Hamilton. Thus, in 1800 Adams lost to Jefferson (although the House had to break a tie between him and his vice-presidential running mate, Aaron Burr) and power passed peacefully to a new administration and party. Yet under Washington's firm leadership the Federalists had made the Constitution a workable instrument of government and established economic policies and principles of foreign affairs (particularly of neutrality) that even Jefferson's Republicans would continue.

KEY EVENTS

1789   *Washington inaugurated:* new government under the Constitution begins

                French Revolution begins: Americans hail movement for liberty in Europe

                Judiciary Act: Supreme Court created

1790   *Funding and assumption:* national government strengthened and public credit restored

1791   *Bank of the United States:* belief government should play an active role in the economy endorsed

                First Ten Amendments (Bill of Rights) ratified: fundamental safeguards of liberty established

1793   *Execution of Louis XVI:* growing radicalism of French Revolution alienates some Americans

                Washington's Neutrality Proclamation: U.S. refuses to aid France in war with Britain

1794   *Whiskey Rebellion:* western farmers resist whiskey tax

1795   *Jay's Treaty:* U.S. tied to Britain economically

                Treaty of Greenville: much of Ohio opened to white settlement

1796   *Pinckney's Treaty:* right to navigate the Mississippi

                Adams elected: first contested presidential election, Washington sets precedent of serving only two terms

1798   *XYZ affair:* French government demands bribe

                Alien and Sedition Acts: Federalists seek to cripple opposition party

                Virginia and Kentucky Resolutions: Madison and Jefferson protest Federalists' interference with civil liberties

1798-1799   *Quasi-War:* naval war with France

1800   *Jefferson defeats Adams:* first national victory by an opposition party

1801   *House elects Jefferson president*

REVIEW QUESTIONS

MULTIPLE CHOICE

1. In 1790, African-Americans made up:
    a. less than 5 percent of the nation's population.
    b. roughly one-fifth of the U.S. population.
    c. nearly half of the U.S. population.
    d. almost three-quarters of the U.S. population.
    (p. 203)

2. In 1789 most Americans:
    a. were semi-subsistence farmers in the trans-Appalachian West.
    b. lived in cities and towns along the coast.
    c. were commercial farmers engaged in international trade.
    d. were outside the commercial economy.
    (p. 203)

3. All of the following were part of Hamilton's program EXCEPT:
    a. prohibiting trade with Britain.
    b. funding and assumption.
    c. a national bank.
    d. a tax on whiskey.
    (pp. 208-209)

4. Critics of Alexander Hamilton feared that his policies:
    a. would create a huge federal deficit.
    b. were too democratic for a republican form of government.
    c. would give too much power to the state governments.
    d. posed a serious threat to Americans' liberties.
    (pp. 209-210)

5. Alexander Hamilton believed the fundamental issue of the Whiskey Rebellion to be:
    a. the power of the states versus the power of the national government.
    b. the constitutional right of elected officials to command militia units.
    c. over the authority of the national government to enforce its policies.
    d. whether the government could prohibit the manufacture of alcohol.
    (p. 212)

6. In response to the French Revolution and the outbreak of war between Britain and France, President George Washington:
    a. declared the United States would maintain its military alliance with France.
    b. proclaimed American neutrality.
    c. formed a military alliance with Britain.
    d. removed Jefferson from his cabinet.
    (p. 215)

7. Jay's Treaty:
    a. officially ended the U.S. alliance with France.
    b. removed all restrictions on American trade with Britain.
    c. was rejected by the Senate.
    d. secured the evacuation of British troops from the Northwest.
    (p. 215)

8. In the XYZ affair:
    a. French officials demanded a bribe to negotiate with the United States.
    b. England agreed to abandon the forts in the Northwest.
    c. Adams broke with his party and sent a new peace commission to France.
    d. the United States agreed to end the Quasi-War.
    (p. 218)

9. In response to the Sedition Act of 1798:
    a. Americans adopted a more absolute view of freedom of speech.
    b. Americans generally believed that strict controls should be placed on newspapers.
    c. South Carolina and Georgia threatened to secede from the Union.
    d. thousands of immigrants left the United States since they would not be able to vote for 14 years.
    (p. 219)

10. The peace treaty John Adams signed with France in 1800:
    a. helped discredit Alexander Hamilton and ensure that Adams would control the Federalist Party.
    b. was violated by both sides.
    c. severely hurt Adams' prospects for reelection.
    d. gained the president the full support of the Federalist Party.
    (p. 219)

11. In 1800, Thomas Jefferson was elected president by the:
  a. Electoral College.
  b. House of Representatives.
  c. people.
  d. state legislatures.
  (p. 220)

12. With the election of 1800, Federalists firmly believed that:
  a. the republic had failed.
  b. their policies had been entrenched and would guarantee the success of the republic.
  c. the Republican policies would ensure the survival of the new nation.
  d. Jefferson would advance the policies of John Adams.
  (p. 220)

COMPLETION

When the _____ went into effect in 1789, the nation's population was overwhelmingly located on the eastern _____ but was rapidly moving into the _____. Most people engaged in _____. Trade was limited by difficulties of _____, which meant that most Americans traded on a _____ system. In the coastal ports, a commercial economy expanded based on transportation by _____, the only cost-effective way to carry goods long distances. Americans such as _____ became known for their commercial values. The biggest supporter of the development of commerce and manufacturing in the Washington administration was _____; his strongest opponent was _____. Jefferson feared that this new economy would introduce _____ into the national character. Hamilton's efforts also created the fear of an _____, and these fears resulted in uprisings such as the _____. These conflicts within the American political system, along with events overseas, led to the creation of _____. The Republicans, the primary opposition movement, feared that governmental power threatened _____. The battles between the two emerging factions grew during the administration of _____, as international incidents such as the _____ Affair and domestic policies such as the _____ Acts added to the rancor. With the triumph of Jefferson in 1800, the _____ Party lost its hold on power.

IDENTIFICATION

You should be able to describe the following key terms, concepts, individuals, and places and explain their significance.

Terms and Concepts

Funding and assumption
Bank of the United States
Implied powers
Pinckney's Treaty
Bill of Rights
Whiskey Rebellion
XYZ Affair
Alien and Sedition Acts

Tariff
Jay's Treaty
Enumerated powers
Washington's Farewell Address
Quasi-War
Judiciary Act of 1789
Virginia and Kentucky Resolutions
Washington's proclamation of neutrality

Individuals and Places

Alexander Hamilton
John Jay
Benjamin Franklin
James Madison

Thomas Jefferson
Hector St. John de Crèvecoeur
John Adams
Aaron Burr

ESSAY

1. What is your life like as a semi-subsistence farmer? Describe and discuss it in terms of both economic and social aspects. What attitude do you take toward government?

2. List three ways Hamilton's program strengthened the Federal government. How did each of these do so specifically? Which do you think was the most important, and why?

3. Name three events that contributed to worsening relations between the United States and France in the 1790s. How did each event you listed strain relations between the two countries?

4. Why did the election of 1800 mark a milestone in the history of the United States? Describe the election, its outcome, and its significance. What were the most important causes of the Federalist party's defeat?

5. How did Federalists and Republicans differ on economic issues? Were economic, constitutional, or foreign policy issues the most important factors in the emergence of political parties in the 1790s?

CRITICAL THINKING

EVALUATING EVIDENCE (MAPS AND ILLUSTRATIONS)

1. In the cartoon on page 216, how are Washington and the Federalist party linked with patriotism? How is Jefferson linked with disloyalty?

2. What indicates that the cartoon on page 216 is a Federalist cartoon? When do you think it was published?

3. In the picture on page 221, what reveals the growing popular participation in politics? What indicates that elections in this period were also a form of popular entertainment? What activities would worry the Federalists?

PRIMARY SOURCE: Hamilton and Jefferson on the Emergence of Parties

In 1792, Alexander Hamilton and Thomas Jefferson both reflected on the emergence of political parties during Washington's first term. Writing to a close friend, Hamilton defended his policies and expressed his resentment of Jefferson's and Madison's opposition. Jefferson's defense of his position, criticizing Hamilton's program, was prompted by a letter from Washington deploring the conflict between his two advisers and urging greater moderation on both sides. The excerpt from Hamilton is first.

> It was not till the last session [of Congress] that I became unequivocally convinced of the following truth—"That Mr. Madison, cooperating with Mr. Jefferson, is at the head of a faction decidedly hostile to me and my administration, and actuated by views, in my judgment subversive of the principles of good government and dangerous to the union, peace, and happiness of the Country."...

> Mr. Jefferson...manifests his dislike of the funding system generally, calling in question the expediency of funding a debt at all....In the question concerning the Bank [of the United States] he not only delivered an opinion in writing against its constitutionality and expediency, but he did it in a style and manner which I felt as partaking of asperity and ill humor towards me....

> In respect to foreign politics, the views of these gentlemen [Jefferson and Madison] are in my judgment equally unsound and dangerous. They have a womanish attachment to France and a womanish resentment against Great Britain. They would draw us into the closest embrace of the former and involve us in all the consequences of her politics, and

they would risk the peace of the country in their endeavors to keep us at the greatest possible distance from the latter....The Neutral and Pacific Policy appear to me to mark the true path to the United States....

I am told serious apprehensions are disseminated in your state as to the existence of a Monarchical party meditating the destruction of State and Republican Government....I assure you,...there is not in my judgment a shadow of foundation of it....As to my own political Creed,...I am affectionately attached to the Republican theory. I desire above all things to see the equality of political rights exclusive of all hereditary distinction firmly established by a practical demonstration of its being consistent with the order and happiness of society....I acknowledge the most serious apprehensions that the Government of the United States will not be able to maintain itself against their [the states'] influence....Hence, a disposition on my part towards a liberal construction of the powers of the National Government....As to any combination to prostrate the State Governments I disavow and deny it....

On the whole, the only enemy which Republicanism has to fear in this Country is the spirit of faction and anarchy. If this will not permit the ends of Government to be attained under it—if it engenders disorders in the community, all regular and orderly minds will wish for a change, and the demagogues who have produced the disorder will make it for their own aggrandizement. This is the old Story.

—From Alexander Hamilton to Edward Carrington, May 26, 1792

That I have utterly, in my private conversations, disapproved of the system of the Secretary of the treasury, I acknowledge and avow; and this was not merely a speculative difference. His system flowed from principles adverse to liberty, and was calculated to undermine and demolish the republic, by creating an influence of his department over the members of the legislature. I saw this influence actually produced, and its first fruits to be the establishment of the great outlines of his project by the votes of the very persons who, having swallowed his bait...had nothing in view but to enrich themselves....

If what was actually doing begat uneasiness in those who wished for virtuous government, what was further proposed was not less threatening to the friends of the Constitution. For, in a Report on the subject of manufactures...it was expressly assumed that the general government has a right to exercise all powers which may be for the general welfare....The object of these plans taken together is to draw all the powers of government into the hands of the general legislature, to establish means for corrupting a sufficient corps in that legislature to…preponderate…and to have that corps under the command of the Secretary of the Treasury for the purpose of subverting step by step the principles of the constitution, which he has so often declared to be a thing of nothing which must be changed.

No man is more ardently intent to see the public debt soon and sacredly paid off than I am. This exactly marks the difference between Colonel Hamilton's views and mine, that I would wish the debt paid tomorrow; he wishes it never to be paid, but always to be a thing where with to corrupt and manage the legislature.…

Such views might have justified some thing more than mere expressions of dissent, beyond which, nevertheless, I never went. Has abstinence from the department committed to me been equally observed by him?…In the case of the two nations with which we have the most intimate connections, France and England, my system was to give some satisfactory distinctions to the former, of little cost to us, in return for the solid advantages yielded us by them; and to have met the English with some restrictions which might induce them to abate their severities against our commerce.…Yet the Secretary of the treasury, by his cabals with members of the legislature, and by high-toned declamation on other occasions, has forced down his own system, which was exactly the reverse.…

…My objection to the constitution was that it wanted a bill of rights…Colonel Hamilton's was that it wanted a king and house of lords. The sense of America has approved my objection and added the bill of rights, not the king and lords.…He wishes the general government should have power to make laws binding the states in all cases whatsoever. Our country has thought otherwise: has he acquiesced?…

—From Thomas Jefferson to George Washington, September 9, 1791

Questions

1. What reasons does Hamilton give for his differences with Jefferson? Does Jefferson list the same reasons in explaining their conflict?

2. What values and principles do Hamilton and Jefferson share in common? On what principles do they differ?

3. How does each man appeal to history and past developments in defending his position?

THE JEFFERSONIAN REPUBLIC

KEYS TO THE CHAPTER

LEARNING OBJECTIVES

When you have finished studying this chapter, you should be able to:

1. Outline Jefferson's political principles and philosophy of agrarianism.

2. Discuss Jefferson's domestic and foreign policies as president, and their relationship to his political principles.

3. Describe the process of western expansion after 1800 and the response of native peoples.

4. Discuss the course of American foreign policy both before and after the War of 1812, in a way that explains causes and consequences of the war.

5. Describe American nationalism after the War of 1812.

THE CHAPTER IN PERSPECTIVE

The heated party battles of the 1790s deeply divided the leaders of the Revolution and caused Americans to fear for the survival of the Republic. In 1801 Thomas Jefferson became the first leader of an opposing party to become president. Jefferson had come to power by opposing Hamilton's and the Federalist party's domestic and foreign policies, and he entered office determined to reverse the policies of the previous decade and preserve an agrarian empire of liberty. Yet once in office he quickly discovered that governing the nation was quite different from leading an opposition party. Jefferson and his successors confronted many of the same problems that had been central to the politics of the previous decade: the government's role in the economy, the West, and American rights and independence in a perilous world of warring superpowers. In the end, they chose policies not so very different from those of the Federalists, policies reflecting a new American consciousness of nationhood.

OVERVIEW

As a young bride, Margaret Bayard Smith witnessed Jefferson's inauguration in the isolated new capital "city" of Washington, D.C. Smith, who was a supporter of the new president, recognized the event as a milestone in the Republic's history, for it marked the first peaceful transfer of power to an opposition party.

Jefferson in Power

The sparse and rustic capital seemed to mirror Jefferson's political philosophy. A complex individual, Jefferson combined an apparent radicalism with a large dose of political realism. He had a strong faith in the people and believed in limited government. Convinced that agriculture nurtured the values necessary to preserve republicanism, he wanted to keep commerce and urbanization distinctly subordinate in the American economy. He sought the rule of republican simplicity, which for him meant the rule of the Republican party alone.

Jefferson found, however, that he confronted much different problems in power than in opposition. On economic questions he increasingly compromised. In particular, though he slashed military spending, he failed to dismantle Hamilton's economic program, which had been so crucial in the original formation of the Republican party. Jefferson's principles yielded to his more pragmatic actions.

Moreover, in another crucial development, the power of the third branch of the federal government grew through establishing the principle of judicial review—the right of the Supreme Court to interpret the constitution. This was the work of Chief Justice John Marshall, a staunch Federalist appointed by John Adams. The Court, led by Marshall, asserted its right to rule whether any laws passed by Congress and state legislatures, or rulings of state courts, were unconstitutional. The landmark case of *Marbury v. Madison* (1803) laid out the principle of judicial review.

Jefferson and Western Expansion

Jefferson viewed western expansion as a means to preserve liberty by keeping agriculture and the values of the semi-subsistence economy dominant. When France suddenly offered to sell the entire Louisiana region to the United States, Jefferson leapt at the chance to double the size of the country, even though he doubted that the federal government had the constitutional authority to acquire territory. Once again, as with his economic policies, practical politics prevailed over ideological purity. Jefferson dispatched an expedition under the leadership of Meriwether Lewis and William Clark to explore the new territory, find a route to the Pacific, and strengthen American claims to Oregon.

Whites and Indians on the Frontier

Meanwhile, whites poured across the Appalachian Mountains into the Ohio Valley—first young unmarried men, then families carving farms out of the woods. The rapid clearing of the forest seriously decreased the animal population, heightened floods and erosion, and spread disease. The mass movement into Indian country put stress on the cultural systems of both white and native. One response was a series of emotional frontier revivals marked the beginning of the Second Great Awakening. The revival camp meetings offered social outlets for isolated pioneer families and respite from life's hardships, as well as a chance to hear a message of hope and individual salvation.

White encroachment and fur trade led to cultural disorder for the Indians as well. And like the pioneer settlers, many rallied to a religious movement. The Shawnee leader Tenskwatawa, known as the Prophet, sought to revitalize Indian cultures by limiting contact with whites, rejecting white goods, and preserving tribal lands. His movement, however, proved unable to prevent further land cessions. The Prophet's prestige was soon eclipsed by his brother Tecumseh, who advocated combining the western and southern tribes in a political and military alliance to protect their lands and way of life.

The Second War for American Independence

Increasingly, foreign affairs dominated American politics. When war resumed between Britain and France in 1805, neither power was willing to respect the United States' rights as a neutral nation, and both began to raid American shipping on the high seas and impress American sailors. American grievances were stronger against Britain, which had the more powerful navy. Reluctant to resort to force, Jefferson tried to use peaceful coercion by imposing an embargo on American trade with both countries. Some areas, especially New England, openly flouted the law, and eventually the Republican party had to abandon this policy.

James Madison, Jefferson's successor, came under mounting pressure from younger nationalistic Republicans, known as War Hawks. The War Hawks were indignant over British interference with American shipping and meddling with the western Indians. When renewed efforts at peaceful coercion and negotiation failed, the United States finally declared war on Britain in order to defend American rights and uphold national independence.

Americans proved woefully ill-prepared for war. Efforts to invade Canada failed dismally, the British occupied Washington and burned a number of government buildings, and only Andrew Jackson's victory at New Orleans redeemed American pride. Meanwhile, Tecumseh allied his followers with the British, seeing such an alliance as the western tribes' best chance to safeguard their lands. His death in battle ended his pan-Indian movement. A Federalist stronghold, New England refused to support the war, and the region's opposition culminated in the Hartford Convention of 1814, which rejected calls for disunion but proposed several constitutional amendments to reduce the South's political influence. The proposals were discredited by news soon after that a treaty had been signed, ending the war.

America Turns Inward

Despite many military failures, New England's opposition, and a treaty that ignored the issues, the war produced several long-term consequences. It broke the power of Tecumseh's movement, opening the way for white settlement of the Northwest. It destroyed the Federalist party, which was hurt by its opposition to the war. And it led to a surge of American nationalism.

This postwar nationalism could be seen in the foreign policy of President James Monroe. A treaty with Spain acquired Florida and established the principle of American expansion to the Pacific, while the Monroe Doctrine proclaimed the New World's independence from Europe. Relations with Britain improved dramatically after 1815. Britain's recognition of American sovereignty ended the threat of foreign meddling in American affairs, bringing to a close the quest to secure independence. America, under a new generation of nationalistic leaders, could turn inward toward continental development. Then, unfortunately, the Missouri crisis exposed a deepening sectional rift.

KEY EVENTS

1790s	*Second Great Awakening begins:* revivals sweep across the frontier
1801	*Adams's last-minute appointments:* controversial Federalist attempt to fill new federal offices
	Marshall becomes Chief Justice: Federalist ideals remain dominant on the Supreme Court
	Jefferson inaugurated in Washington: first opposition candidate to become president
1803	*Marbury v. Madison:* Supreme Court affirms doctrine of judicial review
	Louisiana Purchase
	War resumes between Great Britain and France: American neutral rights again violated
1804-1806	*Lewis and Clark expedition:* exploration of the upper Louisiana Purchase and Oregon

1807	*Chesapeake affair:* British attack on U.S. warship produces public outcry
	Embargo Act passed: provokes open resistance in New England
1808	*Madison elected president*
1809	*Tecumseh's confederacy organized:* advocates political and military alliance to stop white expansion
1810-1813	*West Florida annexed*
1811	*Battle of Tippecanoe:* Prophet's movement undermined
1812	*War declared against Great Britain:* War Hawks push war to defend American independence
1813	*Tecumseh killed:* hopes for Indian confederacy destroyed
1813-1814	*Creek War:* Creeks' military power broken, forcing them to cede a large tract of land
1814	*Hartford Convention:* Federalist party tainted with disunion
	Treaty of Ghent
1815	*Battle of New Orleans*
1818	*Joint occupation of Oregon*
1819	*Transcontinental Treaty:* boundary line with Spain drawn to the Pacific, foreshadowing future U.S. expansion
	United States acquires Florida
1819-1821	*Missouri Crisis*
1823	*Monroe Doctrine:* U.S. opposes further European colonization in the new world

REVIEW QUESTIONS

MULTIPLE CHOICE

1. Once in power, Jefferson:
   - a. completely dismantled Hamilton's economic program.
   - b. appointed John Marshall chief justice.
   - c. announced that he was a Federalist.
   - d. increasingly adopted broad construction.

   (pp. 227-228)

2. Jefferson believed in:
    a. one-party rule
    b. a two-party system that institutionalized a loyal opposition.
    c. a two-party system so long as his party held a majority.
    d. a multi-party system that balanced factional interests.
    (p. 227)

3. As they left office, Federalists hoped to retain influence by:
    a. passing constitutional amendments to limit the power of the president.
    b. redistricting the states to allow for more Federalists in the House of
       Representatives.
    c. expanding the size of the federal court system.
    d. appointing Federalists to important regulatory agencies.
    (p. 228)

4. According to the doctrine established in the landmark Supreme Court case
   Marbury v. Madison:
    a. the Court upheld the doctrine of implied powers.
    b. the Court could rule on the constitutionality of federal laws.
    c. the Court could compel public officials to perform their duties.
    d. the executive branch must defer to the rulings of the legislative branch.
    (p. 228)

5. Jefferson favored western expansion for all of the following reasons EXCEPT:
    a. he thought it would sustain the values necessary in an ideal Republic.
    b. he thought it would strengthen his party.
    c. he thought it would strengthen the power of the federal government.
    d. he thought it would strengthen American economic and security interests.
    (p. 229)

6. In the South of the early 1800s:
    a. strict slave codes prohibited slaves from attending Christian churches.
    b. the Catholic Church led the way in converting African-Americans.
    c. white Southerners feared that revivalists would spread rebellion among
       the slaves.
    d. revivalism was important in spreading Christianity to African-Americans.
    (pp. 233-234)

7. The Shawnee Chief Tecumseh:
      a. created a confederation among northern tribes but not in the South.
      b. failed in his efforts to create an Indian confederation in the Northwest.
      c. won several important military victories, which led to a Pan-Indian confederation.
      d. protected the interests of his tribe by helping the Americans fight the British in 1812.
      (pp. 235-238, 241-242)

8. The Embargo:
      a. especially hurt New England's prosperity.
      b. was widely evaded and thus had little impact on the U.S. economy.
      c. led Napoleon to repeal his economic decrees—but too late to avoid war.
      d. was a last resort after undeclared naval war had failed.
      (pp. 239-240)

9. In 1812, the United States went to war with England for all of the following reasons EXCEPT:
      a. the desire to gain additional territory.
      b. anger over British dealings with Indians.
      c. gaining acceptance as an independent nation.
      d. to honor a treaty obligation to Spain.
      (pp. 238-241)

10. The American victory at the Battle of Horseshoe Bend:
      a. drove the British army out of Baltimore.
      b. prevented the British from capturing Alabama.
      c. resulted in the death of Tecumseh.
      d. destroyed the military power of the Indians in the Old Southwest.
      (p. 242)

11. The Monroe Doctrine:
      a. proclaimed that the U.S. would be a continental nation.
      b. warned Europe not to interfere in the Americas.
      c. guaranteed the independence of Spain's former colonies.
      d. laid claim to the Oregon country for the United States.
      (pp. 246-247)

12. The Missouri Compromise provided for all of the following EXCEPT:
   a. banning slavery in the rest of the Louisiana Purchase north of the southern boundary of Missouri.
   b. the admission of Missouri as a slave state.
   c. the admission of Maine as a free state.
   d. securing a balance of free and slave state-power in the House of Representatives.
   (p. 245)

COMPLETION

Jefferson was the first president to be inaugurated in _____. He called his election _____, although perhaps that is an exaggeration. While he believed in free speech, he did not hesitate to try to _____ judges with whom he disagreed. Similarly, although he claimed he wanted to limit the power of the federal government, events such as the purchase of _____ and the _____ that shut the nation's coastal ports reveal that he was willing to exert federal power when it suited his purposes. Jefferson was fascinated with the West, sending _____ on an expedition up the Missouri River in search of a Northwest Passage. Americans shared his fascination, pouring into the backcountry and changing the _____ through deforestation. Their settlement further infringed on the Indians, who took different approaches to these incursions. _____, a Shawnee chief, advocated adopting the ways of white culture; _____ and his younger brother _____ advocated a return to traditional Indians ways. The latter mirrored the renewed religious interest among whites known as _____. While the Indians struggled to maintain unity, Jefferson attempted to do the same in American politics in the face of yet another war between _____ and _____. These powers violated American _____ rights through raids on ships and _____ of American sailors. Eventually the fear that American independence hung in the balance led to the _____. When this conflict failed to resolve any significant issues, Americans turned inward, gaining new confidence from peace and the glorious victory of _____ in the Battle of New Orleans. Soon, however, the first sectional crisis, known as the _____, introduced the specter of slavery into the forefront of national politics.

IDENTIFICATION

You should be able to describe the following key terms, concepts, individuals, and places and explain their significance.

Terms and Concepts

War of 1812
Louisiana Purchase
Orders in Council
Hartford Convention
Transcontinental Treaty
Judicial review
Treaty of Ghent

Impressment
Embargo
Monroe Doctrine
Camp meeting
Marbury v. Madison
Chesapeake affair

Individuals and Places

Thomas Jefferson
John Quincy Adams
Battle of New Orleans
Oliver Hazard Perry
Napoleon
Tecumseh
John Marshall

James Madison
Andrew Jackson
Battle of Lake Erie
James Monroe
Cane Ridge
The Prophet Tenskwatawa

MAP IDENTIFICATION

On the map, label or shade in the following places. In a sentence, note their significance to the chapter. (For reference, consult the maps on pages 237 and 243 of *Nation of Nations*.)

1. Tippecanoe
2. New Orleans
3. Washington
4. Lake Erie
5. West Florida
6. Creek cession
7. Fort McHenry
8. British invasion routes

East coast to Great Lakes (small)

ESSAY

1. Give several examples of Jefferson's pragmatism. How does each example demonstrate this quality of Jefferson's leadership?

2. What was decided in the case of *Marbury v. Madison*? Why was the case an important one?

3. What issues led to the war between Britain and the United States in 1812? How did each issue contribute to the outbreak of war?

4. Compare the boundaries of the United States in 1800 and 1820. What successive events produced the changes?

5. Compare attitudes of, on the one hand, Jefferson and J. Q. Adams toward the western extension of U.S. control and, on the other hand, those of Black Hoof, the Prophet, and Tecumseh. Which of the two political leaders had the more realistic vision? Which of the native leaders had the most realistic response?

6. Give yourself a location and occupation. Did you support the war against England in 1812? In 1814? In 1815? Why? How were you affected by the war?

7. Why does the text refer to the War of 1812 as the "second war for American independence?" What events *after* the war give proof that this war for independence was successful?

CRITICAL THINKING

EVALUATING EVIDENCE (MAPS AND ILLUSTRATIONS)

1. Why was so little known about the Louisiana Purchase in 1803 (map, page 231)? How far had American settlement reached by then?

2. How did Lewis and Clark strengthen American claims to Oregon (map, page 231)? What did Pike's explorations contribute to American territorial claims?

3. Which tribes were under the greatest pressure from whites in terms of their land holdings (map, page 237)? What was the relationship between the spread of the Prophet's and Tecumseh's movements and Indian land cessions?

4. Which tribes rallied to Tecumseh's movement, according to the map on page 237? Where did he have the greatest success and why?

5. In the scene of a revival (page 234), what indicates that it is a camp meeting? Does the picture present a favorable view of the ministers? Is it sympathetic toward the congregation? How does it portray the activities? Are there important activities omitted?

PRIMARY SOURCE: Tecumseh Confronts Governor Harrison[*]

Alarmed by the Prophet's and Tecumseh's efforts to form an Indian confederacy, Governor William Henry Harrison sent a communication in July 1810 urging peace and warning them of the danger of any war with the United States. Tecumseh told the bearer of the message.

> *The Great Spirit said he gave this great island to his red children. He placed the whites on the other side of the big water. They were not contented with their own, but came to take ours from us. They have driven us from the sea to the lakes. We can go no farther. They have taken upon themselves to say this tract belongs to the Miamis, this to the Delawares, and so on. But the Great Spirit intended it as the common property of all the Tribes, nor can it be sold without the consent of all. Our father tells us that we have no business on the Wabash, the land*

[*] From Logan Esarey, ed., *Messages and Letters of William Henry Harrison.*

belongs to other Tribes, but the Great Spirit ordered us to come here and we shall stay.

Soon afterward Tecumseh journeyed to Vincennes to meet with Harrison. In this conference on August 20 and 21, 1810, Tecumseh outlined the Indians' grievances and demands. His speeches were taken down by an American participant.

> *Brother...after we agreed to bury the Tomahawk at Greenville...the Americans...told us they would treat us well....Since the peace was made you have killed some of the Shawnee, Winnebagoes, Delawares, and Miamis and you have taken our lands from us and I do not see how we can remain at peace with you if you continue to do so....You wish to prevent the Indians to do as we wish them to unite and let them consider their land as the common property of the whole....You are continually driving the red people when at last you will drive them into the great lake where they can't either stand or work.*

> *Brother...Since my residence at Tippecanoe [i.e., Prophetstown] we have endeavored to level all distinctions [in order] to destroy village chiefs by whom all mischief is done; it is they who sell our land to the Americans and our object is to let all our affairs be transacted by Warriors.*

> Brother. *This land that was sold and the goods that were given for it [in the Treaty of Fort Wayne] was only done by a few....These tribes set up a claim [to the land that was sold] but the tribes with me will not agree to their claim. If the land is not restored to us you will soon see when we return to our homes how it will be settled. We shall have a great council at which all the tribes shall be present when we will show to those who sold that they had no right to sell the claim they set up and we will know what will be done with those Chiefs that did sell the land to you. I am not alone in this determination. It is the determination of all the warriors and red people that listen to me.*

> *Now wish you to listen to me. If you do not it will appear as if you wished me to kill all the chiefs that sold you this land. I tell you so because I am authorised by all the tribes to do so. I am at the head of them all....It has been the object of both myself and [my] brother from the beginning to prevent the lands being sold....I am alone the acknowledged head of all the Indians.*

At this point, Harrison asked Tecumseh if government surveyors in the lands ceded by the Treaty of Fort Wayne would be resisted. Tecumseh replied:

Brother. *They [his followers] want to save that piece of land. We do not wish you to take it. It is small enough for our purposes. If you do take it you must blame yourself as the cause of trouble between us and the Tribes who sold it to you. I want the present boundary line [of the Treaty of Greenville] to continue. Should you cross it, I assure you it will be productive of bad consequences.*

Questions

1. Give three specific complaints by Tecumseh about American policy toward the Indian tribes. What examples does he refer to in support of each of these points?

2. How does Tecumseh envision a different relationship between the Indians and the American government? Why is this new relationship unacceptable to American officials?

3. What does Tecumseh see as the ultimate result if the Indian tribes do not unite? Was he correct in this belief?

4. How should Harrison have interpreted Tecumseh's remarks and intentions? Does he seem to be threatening war unless American policy is changed? Is he clear about his intentions?

5. What sense of Tecumseh's character emerges from this document? Does he seem particularly insightful? Does he seem forthright in his remarks? Why do you think whites were so impressed with him?

THE OPENING OF AMERICA

KEYS TO THE CHAPTER

LEARNING OBJECTIVES

When you have finished studying this chapter, you should be able to:

1. Explain the nature of the market revolution and its importance to American economic growth after 1815.

2. Describe the transportation revolution and its impact on the economy.

3. State the role of the Supreme Court in promoting economic growth and investment.

4. Describe the impact of technology, the rise of factories, and the changing lives of workers in this period.

5. Describe the impact of the market revolution on American society and values, with particular attention to economic specialization, the concentration of wealth, the increased discipline of the clock, and the boom-bust cycle.

6. State the terms and significance of the Missouri Compromise.

THE CHAPTER IN PERSPECTIVE

When Washington became the first president of the United States in 1789, American society was divided into a small commercial sector along the seaboard and a larger semi-subsistence economy in the interior. The party battles that erupted in the 1790s reflected competing views of social and economic development. The Federalists hoped to create a commercial nation, while the Jeffersonian Republicans championed an agrarian, semi-subsistence republic. In the quarter-century after 1789, these two parts of the country developed economically and socially independent of one another. As white settlers began pouring across the Mountains, the lack of cheap land transportation prevented the integration of eastern and interior societies. But developments over the next generation would both link the regions together and transform America into an integrated commercial nation.

OVERVIEW

This chapter deals with one of two great transformations in the quarter-century after 1815: the fundamental economic changes that occurred. (The next chapter covers the political revolution.) The career of Chauncey Jerome illustrates the connection between economic developments and changes in American values and society. The new market society depended on a stricter sense of time. By providing inexpensive, mass-produced clocks and aggressively marketing them in the United States and even around the world, Jerome gained fame and wealth. But the ups and downs of his career also demonstrated how fleeting success could be in the new boom-and-bust market economy, as Jerome lost everything near the end of his life and died in poverty.

The Market Revolution

The development of widespread markets fundamentally transformed opportunity in the United States. Government played an important role in initiating this market revolution after the War of 1812. Congress enacted the program known as the "new nationalism," including a protective tariff, a national bank, and federal aid to internal improvements (transportation facilities). The rapid expansion of cotton production in the Deep South, much of which was sold in England, was the most important stimulant to economic growth. Equally crucial was the development of canals, steamboats, and eventually railroads: The resulting transportation revolution for the first time enabled goods to be transported cheaply on land, and encouraged regional specialization in farming. By adopting a pro-business stance that encouraged investment and risk taking, the Supreme Court under John Marshall played a key role as well. Corporations increasingly became an important form of business organization, to which the courts offered special legal protections and encouragement.

A Restless Temper

Economic expansion generated great social energy and restlessness. Eager to succeed in the new competitive markets, Americans were driven by dreams of wealth yet haunted by fears of failure. Population continued to double every 22 years or so. These new Americans were constantly on the move, pouring steadily westward or flocking to the burgeoning cities in search of opportunity. The majority of new western settlers were farmers. In the ensuing land boom, land sales swung up and down with the economy as an unprecedented amount of acreage was sold, largely to speculators. At the same time, truly significant cities developed—not just in the older regions of the country, but in the West as well. Expansion was the keynote of the new America.

The Rise of Factories

As markets developed, entrepreneurs reorganized their operations to increase production. The American factory system developed in the Northeast, beginning with the textile industry. Eventually all operations (from opening the cotton bales to weaving the cloth) were combined on one site, with the work done largely by machines tended by semi-skilled operators. Lowell, Massachusetts, became the center of the textile industry and the symbol of this new mode of production. At first farm girls worked the Lowell mills; eventually Irish immigrants replaced them. The mills depended on water power, and eventually the rivers were badly polluted. Factory work imposed a new discipline, oriented around the clock, which eroded older standards of craftsmanship. Even when no machines were used, the production process was reorganized. The shoe industry, for example, divided production into a series of steps, with workers performing only one distinct step. Some workers protested against these changes by organizing unions, issuing political demands, and going on strike. But the depression that began in 1837 destroyed this embryonic union movement.

Social Structures of the Market Society

Industrialization created a new middle class, and members separated themselves socially and economically from workers. As opportunities for profit expanded, specialization increased—for farmer, worker, businessman, even fur trapper—and wealth became increasingly concentrated at the top of American society. Nevertheless, most white Americans still had the opportunity to improve their status, although their belief in economic opportunity exceeded the reality. Moreover, status increasingly came to depend upon wealth. As a result, Americans frantically pursued material goods and success. And increasingly the clock came to dictate the rhythms of life, in the home as well as the workplace.

Prosperity and Anxiety

Prosperity brought with it anxiety, as Americans feared they would be plunged into poverty by sudden downturns of the economy that were beyond the control of individuals. After 1815 the economy lurched forward in fits and starts, so wealth seemed neither permanent nor secure. The first great economic shock came in 1819.

KEY EVENTS

1790   *Slater's textile mill opens:* beginning of the textile industry

1793   *Eli Whitney invents the cotton gin:* cotton production expands in the lower South

1798   *Whitney develops system of interchangeable parts*

1807   *Fulton's* Clermont *initiates regular steamboat service on the Hudson River*

1810   Fletcher v. Peck

1810-1820   *Cotton boom begins in the South*

1816   *Second Bank of the United States chartered*

                 Protective tariff enacted: stimulus to industrialization

1818-1825   *Erie Canal constructed:* launches the canal age and makes New York City the country's major metropolis

1819   McCulloch v. Maryland: constitutionality of the national bank upheld through doctrine of implied powers

1819-1823   *Panic and depression illustrated boom-bust cycle*

1820   *Lowell mills established:* becomes center of textile industry

1825-1850   *Canal era*

1834   *National Trades Union founded*

1837   *Panic*

1839-1843   *Depression*

1844   *Samuel F. B. Morse sends first telegraphic message:* improved communications

1847   *Rotary printing press invented:* fast, cheap printing

REVIEW QUESTIONS

MULTIPLE CHOICE

1. The New Nationalism, a program designed to promote internal economic development following the War of 1812, was pushed by a group of aggressive young Republican nationalists. It included all EXCEPT:
    a. a protective tariff.
    b. aid to internal improvements.
    c. a national bank.
    d. high new taxes to pay off the war debt.
    (p. 255)

2. The transportation revolution:
    a. lowered the cost of moving goods across land.
    b. was important primarily for reducing the time to ship goods to Europe.
    c. helped develop the East but had little importance in the West.
    d. depended entirely on private investment.
    (pp. 256-257)

3. During the quarter-century after the War of 1812 ended, the major expansive force in the American economy was:
    a. land sales.
    b. cotton production.
    c. textile manufacture.
    d. canal construction.
    (p. 255)

4. As commercial agriculture emerged in the United States, farmers engaged in all of the following EXCEPT:
    a. cultivating more acreage.
    b. marketing their own crops.
    c. adopting scientific farming methods.
    d. conducting transactions in cash.
    (p. 258)

5. In *McCulloch v. Maryland*, the Supreme Court:
    a. gave Maryland the authority to tax the Bank of the United States.
    b. overturned a law creating a state-supported bank in Maryland.
    c. accepted the doctrine of implied powers and expanded the authority of the national government.
    d. used the concept of strict construction to limit the role of the federal government in economic affairs.
    (p. 260)

6. A striking element of American society in the early nineteenth century was:
    a. the desire to establish deep roots in a community.
    b. an emphasis on speed and mobility.
    c. an interest in peace and quiet.
    d. the importance placed on proper manners.
    (pp. 261-263)

7. All of the following help account for the shift to factory production EXCEPT:
    a. a growing accessible market.
    b. the availability of investment capital and credit.
    c. the availability of workers.
    d. inventions that gave the United States a head start over Europeans.
    (pp. 266-267)

8. For workers, the factories at Lowell before 1845 depended on:
    a. children.
    b. young women.
    c. widows.
    d. immigrants.
    (p. 267)

9. The mountain men of the American West were:
    a. not tied to a national economic structure.
    b. malcontents and sociopaths who wanted nothing to do with society.
    c. discontented with industrial society, and they left their factories in the East to escape the market economy.
    d. expectant capitalists who played an active role in the emerging national market economy.
    (pp. 272-273)

10. The Panic of 1819 is significant because it:
    a. marked the last major American depression until 1929.
    b. ended the optimistic nationalism that followed the War of 1812.
    c. delayed the growth of the market economy until after 1865.
    d. created a huge deficit for the national government.
    (p. 277)

COMPLETION

Changes in manufacturing during _____'s lifetime reveal how the _____ affected the development of the American economy. The embargo and the War of 1812 caused the creation of a _____ market. The new leaders were all ardent _____, eager to use federal power to promote economic development. Inventions such as Whitney's _____, Fulton's _____, and Morse's _____ all facilitated this economic change. The courts also supported this trend, with Chief Justice _____ acting aggressively to protect new forms of business such as the _____. The _____ system in Lowell and Lynn forced their workers to adapt to a schedule driven by the clock, rather than producing at their own natural pace. The market economy also led to a tendency toward _____, which heightened as inventors such as Eli Whitney created the concept of _____, allowing workers with less expertise to manufacture goods more quickly. These changes in the workplace led to the rise of an ideology of _____, as well as to the increased separation of the _____ from manual laborers and a more uneven _____ of wealth. The new economy also caused a cycle of _____ in the economy.

IDENTIFICATION

You should be able to describe the following key terms, concepts, individuals, and places and explain their significance.

Terms and Concepts

Boom-bust cycle	Domestic market
Market revolution	Corporations
Interchangeable parts	Clermont
Materialism	Panic of 1819
Erie Canal	National Trades Union
Missouri Compromise	Second Bank of the United States
Paternalism	*McCulloch v. Maryland*
Gibbons v. Ogden	*Fletcher v. Peck*
Dartmouth College v. Woodward	Transportation revolution

Individuals and Places

Eli Whitney

Samuel Slater

Lowell

Lynn

Chauncey Jerome

Samuel F. B. Morse

Boston Associates

John Marshall

MAP IDENTIFICATION

On the map, label or shade in the following places. In a sentence, note their significance to the chapter. (For reference, consult the map on page 259 of *Nation of Nations*.)

1. Erie Canal
2. Mississippi River
3. Ohio River
4. Hudson River
5. New Orleans
6. St. Louis
7. National Road

ESSAY

1. What were the new forms of transportation that developed in the period from 1800 to 1850? Explain why the transportation revolution stimulated the development of a national domestic market.

2. List three ways that the government promoted economic growth after 1815. Provide evidence to show which was the most important.

3. Why did factories develop in the United States? How did they change over time?

4. List three ways that the development of a national market changed American society after 1815. Did these changes make American society more open than before? What does the phrase "opening of America" mean?

5. Pick two of the following personas and, in a diary that covers 20 years, explain the impact of the market economy on "your" lives: a mountain man, a Lowell mill girl, a Lynn shoemaker, a farmer, Chauncey Jerome.

East coast to Great Lakes (large)

CRITICAL THINKING

EVALUATING EVIDENCE (MAPS AND ILLUSTRATIONS)

1. Why were canals concentrated in the North, as the map on page 259 indicates? What form of transportation was critical to the development of commercial agriculture in the Southwest?

2. How does the picture of St. Louis on page 264 illustrate the impact of the market revolution on older communities? If you did not know which city this was, what in

3. In the map of Lowell on page 269, what is the significance of the location of the textile mills? What indicates the importance of water power in the city's development?

4. How does the map on page 269 suggest that Lowell's growth affected people living many miles away?

PRIMARY SOURCE: Reminiscences of a Lowell Mill Worker[*]

After her father's death, Lucy Larcom moved to Lowell in 1835 with her mother, who ran a company boarding house. She went to work in the mills when she was 11 years old in order to help pay family expenses. She held a variety of jobs there during the next 10 years, was a contributor to the *Lowell Offering,* and eventually left the factory to become a teacher and writer. In her autobiography, Larcom recounted some of her experiences at Lowell.

I never cared much for machinery. The buzzing and hissing and whizzing of pulleys and rollers and spindles and flyers around me often grew tiresome. I could not see into their complications, or feel interested in them. But in a room below us we were sometimes allowed to peer in through a sort of blind door at the great waterwheel that carried the works of the whole mill. It was so huge that we could only watch a few of its spokes at a time, and part of its dripping rim, moving with a slow, measured strength through the darkness that shut it in. It impressed me with something of the awe which comes to us in thinking of the great Power which keeps the mechanism of the universe in motion....

The printed regulations forbade us to bring books into the mill, so I made my window-seat into a small library of poetry, pasting its side all over with newspaper clippings....One great advantage which came to these many stranger girls through being brought together, away from their own homes, was that it taught them to go out of themselves, and enter into the lives of others....To me, it was an incalculable help to find myself among so many working-girls, all of us thrown upon our own resources, but thrown much more upon each others' sympathies.

The last window in the row behind me was filled with flourishing house-plants—fragrant-leaved geraniums, the overseer's pets. They gave that corner a bowery look; the perfume and freshness tempted me there often. Standing before that window, I could look across the room and see girls moving backwards and forwards among the spinning-frames, sometimes stooping, sometimes reaching up their arms, as their work

---

[*] From Lucy Larcom, *A New England Girlhood Outlined from Memory* (1889).

required, with easy and not ungraceful movements. On the whole, it was far from being a disagreeable place to stay in. The girls were bright-looking and neat, and everything was kept clean and shining. The effect of the whole was rather attractive to strangers....

I know that sometimes the confinement of the mill became very wearisome to me. In the sweet June weather I would lean far out of the window, and try not to hear the unceasing clash of sound inside. Looking away to the hills, my whole stifled being would cry out, "Oh, that I had wings!" Still I was there from choice, and "The prison unto which we doom ourselves / No prison is."...Even the long hours, the early rising, and the regularity enforced by the clangor of the bell were good discipline for one who was naturally inclined to dally and dream, and who loved her own personal liberty with a willful rebellion against control. Perhaps I could have brought myself into the limitations of order and method in no other way....

I regard it as one of the privileges of my youth that I was permitted to grow up among those active, interesting girls, whose lives were not mere echoes of other lives, but had principle and purpose distinctly their own....They gave me a larger, firmer ideal of womanhood.

I do not believe that any Lowell mill-girl was ever absurd enough to wish to be known as a "factory-lady," although most of them knew that "factory-girl" did not represent a high type of womanhood in the Old World. But they themselves belonged to the New World, not to the Old; and they were making their own traditions, to hand down to their Republican descendants,—one of which was and is that honest work has no need to assert itself or to humble itself in a nation like ours, but simply to take its place as one of the foundation-stones of the Republic.

Questions

1. Are Larcom's recollections about her experiences as a mill worker positive? What did she gain from her experiences in the factory?

2. How has time to reflect on her early life affected her view of this experience? Do you think she felt the same way at the time?

3. What did she like and/or dislike about working in the factory?

4. What bound these working women together? Was there a sense of community? Was it important they came from similar backgrounds?

5. What is the importance of her use of the words "prison" and "slave" in her description of factory work?

6. How do you think Larcom's concept of women's place in society was altered by her factory experiences?

THE RISE OF DEMOCRACY

KEYS TO THE CHAPTER

LEARNING OBJECTIVES

When you have finished studying this chapter, you should be able to:

1. Describe the new democratic system of politics and give the reasons for its emergence in the 1820s, distinguishing between the policies and supporters of the Democrats and Whigs.

2. Explain the relationship between equality and opportunity, and the importance of these values in the new democratic political system.

3. Explain the status of Indians and blacks in the Jacksonian period, and the relationship of racism to democratic politics.

4. Explain the nullification crisis and the development of the nationalist and state sovereignty interpretations of the Constitution.

5. Explain the significance of the banking issue and its impact on the development of the Jacksonian party system.

THE CHAPTER IN PERSPECTIVE

The development of a national market after 1815 transformed the American economy and society. But a second series of fundamental changes accompanied the market revolution: political changes that are often referred to as the rise of democracy. Democracy had not been valued particularly highly by the Revolutionary generation. To be sure, the United States in 1789 had widespread suffrage by European standards. But politics in the early Republic, despite the attack on aristocracy (Chapter 7), still exhibited a strong elitist strain. Leadership remained in the hands of economic and social elites, appeals to the masses were restrained, popular participation—though increasing—was limited, and politics played only a minor role in most people's lives. All of this changed in the Jacksonian period, as the earlier, more restrained style of politics gave way to the exuberant spirit of democracy.

OVERVIEW

Franklin Plummer was one politician whose public career mirrored the features of the new democratic politics. Born in New England without the advantages of society, Plummer rose to power in Mississippi by portraying opponents as aristocratic snobs. A brilliant if unscrupulous campaigner, Plummer knew how to cater to popular tastes and portray himself as one of the people. His rise and eventual fall (when he began to act like an aristocrat himself) illustrated how profoundly American politics had changed into a more participatory enterprise, and suggested that the new politics of equality bore an uneasy relationship to the new opportunities of the market.

Equality and Opportunity

While European visitors professed shock at American egalitarianism, expanded economic opportunity actually challenged the concept of equality because it allowed some citizens to become much richer than others. Thus this generation had to confront a fundamental tension between two basic American values: opportunity and equality. The democratic party system sought to preserve both equality *and* opportunity by defining equality to mean equality of opportunity, not condition, and safeguarding opportunity through government power.

The Political Culture of Democracy

The new emphasis on democracy arose in response to the Panic of 1819, as voters demanded that their representatives carry out policies to sustain their economic well-being. This new political culture was symbolized by Andrew Jackson. Jackson lacked the experience of typical presidential candidates, but his strong showing in the 1824 election, when he finished first in the popular vote, established his popularity. Though he finally lost the election, his supporters, taking the name Democrats, charged that a "corrupt bargain" had stolen the election. The winner, John Quincy Adams, and his ally Henry Clay would later become founders of the new Whig party.

Demands mounted for a more open and responsive political system. Politics seemed more relevant to people's lives, and as a result popular participation in elections soared. The new political culture of democracy rested on acceptance of political parties as essential for the working of the constitutional system. Parties were pragmatic organizations by which competing interests sought power, while politics itself became mass entertainment.

Jackson's Rise to Power

Personally cold and stiff, John Quincy Adams resisted popular campaigning. In 1828 Jackson defeated Adams for the presidency by exploiting the new politics: portraying himself as a representative of the people in a personality-oriented campaign. Indian removal, the tariff, and banking were the three major problems Jackson confronted as president.

Democracy and Race

Democracy ironically strengthened racism in American society. Essentially excluded from the new democratic system, African-Americans and Indians found their position and rights seriously deteriorating. Eastern Indians, even those that had adopted white ways, were dispossessed of their lands and forced to migrate to new lands across the Mississippi. Free black Americans in the North led lives of hardship and exclusion. Democracy and racism were linked, in part because racism offered whites a refuge from the uncertainties of living in a market-oriented, supposedly egalitarian society.

The Nullification Crisis

Democracy also raised the question of how to reconcile competing economic interests. The problem emerged most clearly in the nullification crisis, when South Carolina, economically depressed and fearful about the future of slavery, endorsed Calhoun's theory of nullification. Calhoun argued that states, as independent members of a constitutional "compact," could nullify federal laws or even secede from the Union. Jackson countered that the Union was perpetual and nullification was illegal. In the end a compromise, hammered out by Clay and Calhoun, gradually lowered the tariff, easing the crisis.

The Bank War

Thirdly, democracy allowed those hurt by the Panic of 1819 to find a scapegoat: the Second Bank of the United States. Once he became president, Jackson moved to destroy it. He feared the great power wielded by the bank, which was controlled by private investors, over state banks and the national economy. Although the bank's president, Nicholas Biddle, exercised his clout responsibly, Jackson vetoed a bill rechartering the bank. He then crippled the bank further by refusing to deposit federal funds (as was required by law) in the bank.

His triumph in the "Bank War" demonstrated how Jackson greatly strengthened the office of the presidency. He used the veto power to control Congress, insisting that he as President was the people's champion.

Van Buren and Depression

Martin Van Buren, Jackson's hand-picked successor, took office just as the nation entered a severe depression. Most of Van Buren's term was devoted to economic questions, which he dealt with ineffectually. Blaming the Democrats for the hard times and exploiting the new democratic politics, the Whigs, organized by Henry Clay as an anti-Jackson movement advocating nationalistic economic policies, gained national power in 1840 for the first time.

The Jacksonian Party System

Democrats and Whigs differed in their attitudes toward the new market economy, how active government should be, and the role of government in fostering the country's moral welfare. Democrats feared the commercialization of American society and wanted government to guard against monopolies and not interfere with individuals' moral beliefs. Whigs, on the other hand, were more comfortable with the mechanisms of the market, advocated an active government to promote economic growth, and insisted that the morals of society be regulated. Whigs were stronger among the business class, but both drew support from workers and farmers. Attitudes toward the market, rather than wealth, distinguished Whigs from Democrats. Democratic efforts to escape the consequences of the market, while preserving its benefits and wealth, were doomed. There was no rolling back the market—or democracy.

KEY EVENTS

1819-1823	*Panic and depression:* popular demand for relief strengthens democratic reform movement
1823	*Biddle becomes president of the Bank of the United States:* bank expands operations in the economy
1825	*House elects John Quincy Adams president:* Jackson's supporters charge a "corrupt bargain"
1828	*Tariff of Abominations:* increase gives no relief to South
	South Carolina Exposition and Protest: doctrine of nullification outlined
	Jackson elected president: new democratic politics
1830	*Webster-Hayne debate:* nationalist and states' rights theories of the Union discussed
1830-1838	*Indians removed from Southeast*

1832	Worcester v. Georgia: Supreme Court rules in favor of the Cherokees but Jackson ignores the ruling
	Jackson vetoes recharter of the national bank: becomes major issue in the presidential election
	South Carolina nullifies tariff: confrontation between state and Jackson threatens the country
	Jackson's Proclamation on Nullification: enunciates the theory of a perpetual union
1833	*Force Bill:* threatens coercion against South Carolina
	Tariffs reduced: compromise ends the nullification crisis
	Jackson removes deposits from the Bank of the United States: movement to destroy the bank
1834	*Whig party organized*
1835-1842	*Second Seminole war:* Seminoles removed by force
1836	*Van Buren elected president:* Democrats retain national power
1837	*Panic:* warning of impending economic crash
1838	*Trail of Tears:* Cherokees removed to the West
1839-1843	*Depression:* Van Buren and Democrats blamed
1840	*Independent Treasury:* replaces national bank

REVIEW QUESTIONS

MULTIPLE CHOICE

1. An irony of the decades after 1820 was that:
   a. the United States was becoming more stratified economically while developing a political system that stressed equality.
   b. more people in the United States had the chance to get rich while at the same time they had fewer opportunities to participate in politics.
   c. farmers who had previously been engaged in subsistence agriculture became the richest group in America.
   d. poor people often voted for wealthy candidates, while rich people tended to support candidates who were common men.
   (p. 283)

2. Many Europeans who traveled to the United States in the first half of the nineteenth century:
   a. expressed surprise that Americans' manners were not much different from the manners of Europeans.
   b. found that Americans treated each other rudely, but they treated foreigners with deference and respect.
   c. were favorably impressed by the way Americans treated all people with politeness and respect.
   d. were often shocked by the rudeness and poor manners of Americans.
   (p. 282)

3. All of the following were democratic reforms of the 1820s EXCEPT:
   a. the popular election of presidential electors.
   b. the emergence of nominating conventions.
   c. the use of secret ballots.
   d. the elimination of property requirements to hold office.
   (p. 285)

4. In the presidential election of 1824:
   a. John Quincy Adams won re-election to a second term.
   b. the Whigs defeated the Democrats, who backed Andrew Jackson.
   c. the House of Representatives chose the president, electing the candidate who came in second in both the popular and electoral votes.
   d. John Calhoun finished second in the popular vote and became vice president.
   (p. 284)

5. To prevent removal, the Cherokees:
   a. appealed to the Supreme Court.
   b. preserved their traditional way of life.
   c. waged a costly war against the United States.
   d. followed the lead of Black Hawk.
   (pp. 290-293)

6. During the Jacksonian era, free blacks in the North:
   a. could not vote in any state.
   b. were subject to segregation.
   c. found jobs in minstrel shows.
   d. were subject to the same laws as whites.
   (pp. 293-295)

7. In the face of economic hardships during the 1820s, South Carolinians increasingly blamed their problems on:
   a. the federal tariff.
   b. high income taxes.
   c. the Republican party.
   d. Henry Clay.
   (p. 296)

8. Calhoun's theory of nullification:
   a. advanced the idea of a perpetual union.
   b. was never put into operation because the southern states opposed it.
   c. argued that the Union was a compact of sovereign states.
   d. upheld the right of the Supreme Court to interpret the Constitution.
   (p. 297)

9. The Second Bank of the United States:
   a. was opposed by business leaders because it restrained economic growth.
   b. was controlled by the federal government.
   c. used its power to drive all state bank notes out of circulation.
   d. used its power to regulate the amount of credit in society.
   (pp. 299-301)

10. Jackson destroyed the national bank by:
    a. refusing to continue to deposit federal funds in it.
    b. precipitating an economic panic in 1833.
    c. getting Congress to pass a new law authorizing him to withdraw all federal funds from it.
    d. issuing the Specie Circular refusing to accept paper money.
    (pp. 300-301)

11. When a depression began in 1837, Van Buren responded by:
    a. lifting restrictions on state bank notes in order to increase the number in circulation.
    b. issuing the Specie Circular.
    c. chartering a new national bank.
    d. calling for establishment of an independent Treasury.
    (pp. 301-302)

12. The presidential campaign of 1840 had special significance because it:
    a. demonstrated the importance of party principles in carrying a national election.
    b. marked the final transition from deferential to egalitarian politics.
    c. restored deferential politics to the American electoral system.
    d. showed that appealing to the common man did not work.
    (pp. 302-304)

COMPLETION

In the 1820s and 1830s, European visitors became more aware of the growing _____ quality of American life. The election of _____ became the most crowded to date in American history, with _____ eventually winning in what supporters of Andrew Jackson called a _____. Four years later, Jackson swept into office, signaling the beginning of the politics of the _____. Democratic sentiment frowned upon privilege and aristocracy, opposing such organizations as the _____. Jackson showed his opposition to privilege in his conduct of the _____ against Nicholas Biddle, but in other ways his administration did not show the same respect for _____. Jackson refused to honor the Supreme Court's decision in *Worcester v. Georgia.* Instead, he ordered the _____ off their land, forcing them to walk the _____ from Georgia to Oklahoma. Nor did Jackson provide support for _____, who were regularly discriminated against and despised for their willingness to work as _____ during labor disputes. Jackson's inclination toward hard stands arose again during the _____ crisis in South Carolina. This time he forced the state to back down from its refusal to honor _____. The defeat of Jackson's successor, _____, in 1840 marked the first national victory for the _____ Party, in what has been called one of the earliest modern _____ because of its use of parades, barbecues, and songs to stir up enthusiasm for the candidates.

IDENTIFICATION

You should be able to describe the following key terms, concepts, individuals, and places and explain their significance.

Terms and Concepts

Removal of the deposits
Indian removal
White manhood suffrage
King Caucus
Segregation
Force bill
Nationalism
Nullification Proclamation
American System

The Bank war
Trail of Tears
King Andrew I
Compromise of 1833
Webster-Hayne debate
Specie Circular
The spoils system
Calhoun's theory of Nullification
Independent Treasury

Individuals and Places

Nicholas Biddle
Martin Van Buren
John Ross
Roger Taney
Henry Clay
John Quincy Adams

Robert Hayne
Andrew Jackson
John C. Calhoun
William Henry Harrison
Denmark Vesey
Daniel Webster

MAP IDENTIFICATION

On the map on the following page, label or shade in the following places. In a sentence, note their significance to the chapter. (For reference, consult the map on page 292 of *Nation of Nations*.)

1. Georgia
2. Cherokee lands in South
3. Creek lands in South
4. Choctaw lands in South
5. Chickasaw lands in South
6. Seminole lands in South
7. New lands of southern tribes
8. Trail of Tears

South (large)

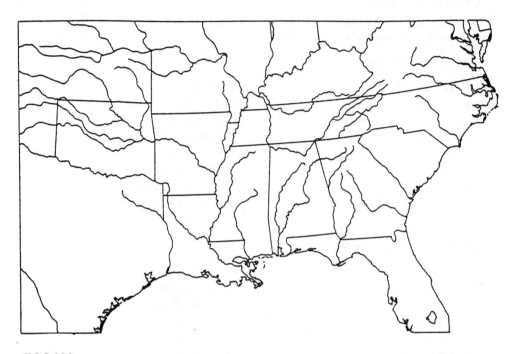

ESSAY

1. List four components of the new democratic political system. How did each of these represent a change from the previous political system?

2. What was Calhoun's theory of nullification? Explain how and why, according to Calhoun's theory, a law could be nullified. Explain how and why nationalists like Webster and Jackson argued against the theory.

3. What powers did the Second Bank of the United States possess that would help it regulate state banks and affect the economy? Why then was Andrew Jackson hostile to the Bank?

4. Write a ballad describing the Cherokee removal.

5. List three political techniques employed by Franklin Plummer of Mississippi that illustrated the new democratic political system. In what sense could he be considered a product of democracy?

CRITICAL THINKING

EVALUATING EVIDENCE (MAPS AND ILLUSTRATIONS)

1. Why does the map of Indian removal (page 292) emphasize the removal of southern tribes? How were they different from northern tribes that suffered the same fate?

2. What features of the new democratic political system are illustrated in the painting of the county election (page 287)? Is this painting critical of democracy? Why or why not?

3. What indicates that the cartoon on the Panic of 1837 (page 298) is a Whig cartoon? What distress does it portray? How does it link this distress to the policies of the Democratic Party? What is its main political message?

PRIMARY SOURCE: A European Nobleman Encounters American Republicanism*

In describing her travels in the United States, Frances Trollope reported the following experience of the Duke of Saxe-Weimar, who toured this country from 1825 to 1826. The well-mannered Duke, she maintained, "could not escape the dislike which every trace of gentlemanly feeling is sure to create among the ordinary class of Americans." Terming such behavior "a national degradation," she condemned the American habit of putting down all aristocratic pretensions.

> *A correspondent of the Charlestown Gazette tells an anecdote connected with the Duke of Saxe-Weimar's recent journey through our country....The scene occurred on the route between Augusta and Milledgeville; it seems that the sagacious Duke engaged three or four, or more seats in the regular stage for the accommodation of himself and suite, and thought by this that he had secured the monopoly of the vehicle. Not so, however; a traveller came along, and entered his name upon the book, and secured his seat by payment of the customary charges. To the Duke's great surprise, on entering the stage, he found our traveller comfortably housed in one of the most eligible seats, wrapped up in his fearnought [i.e., woolen coat], and snoring like a buffalo. The Duke, greatly irritated, called for the question of consideration. He demanded, in broken English, the cause of the gross intrusion, and insisted in a very princely manner, though not, it seems, in very princely language, upon the incumbent vacating the seat in which he had made himself so impudently at home.*

---

* From Frances Trollope, *Domestic Manners of the Americans*, (1832).

But the Duke had yet to learn his first lesson of republicanism. The driver was one of those sturdy southrons, who can always, and at a moment's warning, whip his weight in wild cats: and he as resolutely told the Duke that the traveller was as good, if not a better man than himself, and that no alteration of the existing arrangement could be permitted. Saxe-Weimar became violent at this opposition, so unlike any to which his education had ever subjected him, and threatened John with the application of the bamboo....Down leaped our driver from his box, and peeling himself for the combat, he leaped about the vehicle in the most wild-boar style, calling upon the prince of a five-acre patch to put his threat in execution. But he of the star refused to make up [the] issue in the way suggested, contenting himself with assuring the enraged southron of a complaint to his excellency the Governor, on arrival at the seat of government. This threat was almost as unlucky as the former, for it wrought the individual for whom it was intended into that species of fury which, though discriminating in its madness, is nevertheless without much limit in its violence, and he swore that the Governor might go to —, and for his part he would just as leave lick the Governor as the Duke; he'd like no better fun than to give both Duke and Governor a dressing in the same breath; could do it, he had little doubt, &c. &c.; and instigating one fist to diverge into the face of the marvelling and panic-stricken nobleman, with the other he thrust him down into a seat alongside the traveller, whose presence had been originally of such sore discomfort to his excellency, and bidding the attendants jump in with their discomfited master, he mounted his box in triumph, and went on his journey.

Questions

1. What attitudes and assumptions does the Duke of Saxe-Weimar hold concerning the proper ordering of society? How do his attitudes differ from those of the stagecoach driver?

2. Why does the writer use the term "republicanism" in describing the driver's behavior? What does the author mean by saying that this incident was a lesson in republicanism?

3. What is the relationship between the driver's attitudes about social equality and his views about political equality? How do these attitudes reinforce one another? What does this account say about the nature of politics in the Jacksonian era?

4. Why did European visitors react so strongly to the popular attitudes illustrated in this story? How would an American interpret this scene?

5. What value do European travel accounts have for historians?

4. Why did European visitors react so strongly to the popular attitudes illustrated in this story? How would an American interpret this scene?

5. What value do European travel accounts have for historians?

THE FIRES OF PERFECTIONISM

KEYS TO THE CHAPTER

LEARNING OBJECTIVES

When you have finished studying this chapter, you should be able to:

1. Discuss the nature of the revival of the Second Great Awakening and its impact on both American religion and American society.

2. Discuss the concept of women's sphere, and how women's lives and social role changed in this period.

3. Describe the romantic movement and its impact on American values.

4. Discuss the nature of the antebellum reform movements, including the utopian communities and the humanitarian reform movements.

5. Describe the emergence of abolitionism in American society and its significance.

6. State the impact of reform on the party system, and explain the shift to political action among some reformers.

THE CHAPTER IN PERSPECTIVE

The market revolution (Chapter 10) and the democratic revolution (Chapter 11) were accompanied by a third kind of transformation. The rise of democracy in the Jacksonian era was only one indication of a deeper impulse to improve American society. Equally important were the various reform movements of the period. These grew out of the religious changes that began on the frontier around the turn of the century and flowered in emerging market towns in the 1820s and 1830s. The revivalists' new methods of converting "sinners"—as well as reformers' more direct attempts to perfect society—addressed many problems that were directly connected to the expansion of the economy and the dislocation experienced by many Americans during the market revolution. The mixture of religious revivalism and perfectionist reform added to the new democratic politics and an expanding commercial economy to create an unusual ferment in American society in the years after 1820.

OVERVIEW

The Jacksonian era witnessed immense and profound social changes. Not by coincidence, it also witnessed the greatest number of significant reform movements in American history. Women dominated church membership and played a critical role in those reform movements. Many leaders of reform were inspired by Protestant Christianity's millennial vision. The chapter opens with Lyman Beecher, who along with his children was destined to play such a large role in many of the movements striving for perfection. Beecher viewed religion and reform as forces of stability, yet he anticipated that faithful Christians could bring in the Kingdom of God, and his children increasingly advocated ways to liberate the individual. In short, religion and reform could become both agents of control and also forces for social change. The varied activities of Beecher and his children thus illustrated the close ties between reform and religion, the diversity of the reform impulse, and its growing radicalism.

Revivalism and the Social Order

The reform movements sometimes sought to preserve social institutions, sometimes to overturn them. They drew upon two intellectual developments: revivalism and romanticism. The Second Great Awakening, led by revivalists like Charles Grandison Finney, preached the doctrine of salvation for all sinners who would exercise their free will and choose it. Spurred on by this optimistic message, revivalists eventually endorsed the ideals of perfectionism (that individuals and society could become perfect) and millennialism (that the reign of 1,000 years of peace on earth prophesied in the Bible was at hand). Finney promoted techniques to convert sinners—"new measures" originally used in frontier camp meetings. His revivals helped people adjust to the new market economy and the pressures they experienced in their daily lives by giving them hope and the internal discipline necessary for success. The number of independent black churches increased as well. Revivals strengthened the American belief in equality and individualism and made evangelical Protestantism the dominant expression of religion in America.

Women's Sphere

Women made up the greater number of converts at these revivals. Changes in women's world—men working outside the home, fewer arranged marriages—increased the unpredictability of life and led to a view of women as society's moral guardians. Women's role increasingly centered on home and the family—the ideal of domesticity. Women themselves asserted that women, being morally stronger than men, could guard the nation's future by managing the home, their sphere. To shape society, they therefore turned to religion and reform. For example, as the market revolution and industrialization created a new middle class, families embraced a greater concern for privacy and adopted new techniques to assure the success of their children, including reduced family size, greater education, and equal inheritance and began to adopt practices that increasingly separated home and family from society.

American Romanticism

A new outlook known as Romanticism also stimulated the quest for perfectionism. An intellectual movement that began in Europe, romanticism emphasized the unlimited potential of each individual. It viewed emotion and intuition as sources of truth. Romanticism undergirded a distinct American literature that wrestled with questions about the source of truth and the clash between the individual and society. Ralph Waldo Emerson was the leading romantic thinker of the age. He embraced Transcendentalism, an intensely individualistic philosophical movement that sought to rise above the rational and material. The romantic movement produced a number of major writers who explored, with uniquely American voices, some of the complexities and contradictions of American culture.

The Age of Reform

Some reformers turned to utopian communities to build a model society for the rest of the world to follow. Many—the Shakers, the Oneida community, and the Mormon settlement at Nauvoo—were based in religion; others, like the community at New Harmony, were secular and socialist in their orientation. All believed in being able to perfect human character and remove evil from society. Other reformers turned to humanitarian movements that sought not to withdraw but to attack social evils directly. Movements like temperance, educational reform, and the establishment of asylums all gained support and typified the approach of perfecting society by reforming individuals. Each reflected aspects of both liberation and control.

Abolitionism

In the long run, the most important humanitarian reform movement of the period was abolitionism. William Lloyd Garrison, a Boston editor, laid the ideals and program— "immediatism" and "moral suasion"—of the abolitionist movement, and his views would later cause its breakup. Viewing slavery as the greatest sin in the Republic, abolitionists reflected the influence of the Christian revivals. Other important leaders helped mobilize the abolitionist movement, including Lewis Tappan, James Birney, Theodore Dwight, and free African-Americans in the north like Fredrick Douglass. Abolitionism drew on the crusading idealism of the revivals and the ideals of millennialism and perfectionism. Yet abolitionism attacked powerful groups in American society and championed African-Americans in the face of a pervasive racism. In doing so, abolitionism precipitated strong and often violent opposition. Abolitionists always remained a small minority of northern society.

Abolitionism attracted considerable support from women who were active in church work. Eventually several prominent female abolitionists, led by Elizabeth Cady Stanton and Lucretia Mott, launched the women's rights movement at the Seneca Falls convention in 1848. Drawing a parallel between the oppression of women and slaves, they called for greater educational and employment opportunities for women, enhanced legal rights in marriage, and most controversially the right to vote. The women's rights movement reflected growing internal divisions in the abolitionism. In 1840 the movement split into Garrison's radical wing and a more conservative wing, led by Tappan, that sought to end slavery through the political process.

Reform Shakes the Party System

The Tappan wing of abolitionism was typical in turning to political action. Advocates of temperance as well as antislavery sought to achieve their goals by passing legislation; women reformers thus focused on gaining the right to vote. The passage of the first statewide prohibition law in Maine in 1851 prompted the drive to pass similar laws in other states. The intrusion of these moral questions increasingly disrupted the two national parties; antislavery in particular made it difficult to preserve support in both sections of the country. The party system was weakened.

KEY EVENTS

1787	*First Shaker commune established*
1794	*African-American Bethel Church organized*
1824	*New Harmony established*
1824-1837	*Peak of revivals*
1826	The Last of the Mohicans *published*
	American Temperance Society founded
1830	Book of Mormon *published*
1830-1831	*Finney's revival at Rochester*
1831	The Liberator *commences publication:* Garrison outlines new program of abolitionism
1833	*American Anti-Slavery Society founded*
	Oberlin College admits women
1834	*Lane Seminary rebellion*
1836	*Gag rule passed:* stimulates concern over civil liberties

1837	*Massachusetts establishes state Board of Education:* strengthens educational reform movement
	Emerson's address, "The American Scholar": call for independent national literature
	Mount Holyoke Seminary: first women's college
	Elijah Lovejoy killed: anti-abolitionist violence
1838	*Sarah Grimké's* Letters on the Condition of Women and the Equality of the Sexes *published:* major document in the origins of feminism
1839	*Nauvoo founded*
1840	*Schism of American Anti-Slavery Society:* abolitionist movement crippled by internal divisions
	Liberty Party founded: first antislavery third party
1843	*Dorothea Dix's report:* movement for humane treatment of the insane
1844	*Gag rule repealed:* major victory for antislavery forces
1848	*Oneida Community established*
	Seneca Falls Convention: women's rights movement
1850	*Nathaniel Hawthorne's* The Scarlet Letter *published*
1851	*Maine adopts statewide prohibitory law:* inaugurates drive for similar laws in other states
1854	*Henry David Thoreau's* Walden *published*
1855	*Walt Whitman's* Leaves of Grass *published*

REVIEW QUESTIONS

MULTIPLE CHOICE

1. The reform efforts of the 1820s and 1830s emerged:
    a. in response to the economic and social changes of Jacksonian America.
    b. because the stability of the era gave Americans the opportunity to reflect on the need for moral reform.
    c. when President Andrew Jackson began to encourage Americans to restore their traditional values.
    d. as an effort by political leaders to limit the influence of church leaders on American society.
    (p. 310)

2. The revivals of the Second Great Awakening upheld the doctrine that:
   a. men and women were predestined to salvation or damnation.
   b. salvation was available to all.
   c. only women should be religious.
   d. religion was a way to become wealthy.
   (pp. 310-311)

3. The new middle-class family:
   a. was more prosperous because of dual income of husband and wife.
   b. was larger because increased prosperity allowed parents to support more children.
   c. made sacrifices for the education of daughters so they could be successful and take care of themselves.
   d. was smaller and based on the idea of privacy.
   (pp. 316-317)

4. The ideal of domesticity:
   a. held that women's sphere was the home and family.
   b. was opposed by the revivalists because it took women away from religion.
   c. was strongest among working-class women, who wanted to quit their jobs and stay at home.
   d. stressed the father's spiritual leadership in the home.
   (pp. 314-316)

5. Transcendentalists believed that:
   a. reason and rationalism allowed humans to transcend intellectual limits.
   b. the best way to transcend the sinful world was to live and work in cooperative congregations.
   c. the final judgment day was at hand and human beings needed to prepare to transcend to heaven.
   d. humans had a spark of divinity that let them transcend the material world.
   (p. 318)

6. Romanticism:
   a. came from Europe as part of the Enlightenment.
   b. was incompatible with the doctrines of the revivals.
   c. considered emotion the source of truth.
   d. valued education as the essential means to discover truth.
   (p. 317)

7. The Oneida community:
    a. was based on the principle of sexual equality.
    b. was an extreme example of the doctrine of perfectionism.
    c. lasted only a few years before disbanding.
    d. bankrupted its founder.
    (p. 321)

8. The Mormon Church:
    a. appealed to poor people who rejected materialism.
    b. was founded in 1839 by Joseph Smith at Nauvoo.
    c. sought to re-establish the ancient church.
    d. rejected both evangelicalism and millennialism.
    (pp. 321-322)

9. The temperance movement enjoyed the success it did for all the following reasons EXCEPT:
    a. it received support from the federal government.
    b. it strongly appealed to women.
    c. it reflected the ideals of democratic capitalism.
    d. temperance helped achieve upward mobility.
    (pp. 322-323)

10. The educational reform movement:
    a. led to the establishment of high schools throughout the country.
    b. was supported by businessmen but opposed by workers.
    c. was most successful in the South.
    d. believed tax-supported public schools would promote equal opportunity.
    (p. 323)

11. The abolitionist movement split in 1840:
    a. because of Garrison's support for black rights.
    b. because the movement was bankrupt and could not pay its debts.
    c. over the issue of women's rights.
    d. because of the Liberty party's strong showing in 1839.
    (pp. 328-336)

12. By 1840, the reform movement had:
    a. helped pull the different sections of the nation together.
    b. angered Westerners who did not want to pay taxes to support reforms.
    c. revealed that New England was a moralistic region different from the rest of the nation.
    d. helped highlight differences between the North and the South.
    (pp. 331-333)

COMPLETION

As society during the Jacksonian era underwent deep and rapid changes, many Americans sought _____ and moral order in _____. Evangelical _____, such as the ones led by Charles Grandison Finney, reinforced unity, strength, and discipline. They also spread the doctrine of _____, which argued that humans could make themselves as perfect as God. These gatherings particularly appealed to the _____, who felt intense pressure from the emergence of the market economy. The new economic order brought other pressures to bear on _____, whose new role was to create a place of _____ for men as a haven from the pressures of the outside world. Other responses to the changes in society included _____, an American version of ideology of Romanticism, which was popularized by _____. _____ communities such as New Harmony and Oneida tried to reform the world, while the _____ movement sought to directly change the heavy drinking habits of many Americans. As reform movements became politically active, the issue that emerged most prominently was _____, led by the head of the American Anti-Slavery Society and editor of the *Liberator,* _____. After the _____ convention in 1848, the abolitionist movement split over the issue of women's rights. Yet it remained the most potentially divisive issue within American society. Differences between the two sections of the nation grew during the 1840s and 1850s.

IDENTIFICATION

You should be able to describe the following key terms, concepts, individuals, and places and explain their significance.

Terms and Concepts

Second Great Awakening	Evangelicalism
Liberty party	Domesticity
Perfectionism	Gag law
New measures	Millennialism
Transcendentalism	Romanticism
Women's sphere	Maine law
The Liberator	Moral suasion
Abolitionism	American Anti-Slavery Society

Individuals and Places

William Lloyd Garrison

Dorothea Dix

Charles Grandison Finney

Richard Allen

New Harmony Oneida Community

Joseph Smith

James Birney

Shakers

Frederick Douglass

Elijah Lovejoy

Sarah Grimké

Lucy Stone

Nathaniel Hawthorne

Herman Melville

Walt Whitman

Mount Holyoke

Lyman Beecher

Theodore Dwight Weld

Horace Mann

John Humphrey Noyes

African Methodist Episcopal Church

Seneca Falls convention

Robert Owen

Nauvoo

Elizabeth Cady Stanton

Ralph Waldo Emerson

Ann Lee

Harriet Tubman

Angelina Grimké

Lucretia Mott

Henry David Thoreau

James Fenimore Cooper

Benjamin Lundy

ESSAY

1. What is the millennium? How did millennialism encourage the cause of reform?

2. Define "romanticism." How did the romantic movement contribute to American values? How did it strengthen the reform impulse?

3. Describe the range of antislavery positions and cite at least three people who exemplified those different positions. If you had been a reformer in the 1840s, how would you have felt about the abolitionists and which faction would you have supported? Why?

4. Do you believe the "ideal of domesticity" helped or hurt the position of women in American society? Support your argument with specific examples of how the new ideal affected women's lives.

5. Historians have seen the reform movements of the 1830s and 1840s as both conservative and radical. Give at least two specific examples of how different aspects of these movements were conservative (that is, how they upheld institutions and values). Then suggest at least two examples of how other aspects were radical (that is, how they overturned institutions and values). On balance, was reform a greater force for change or for preservation?

CRITICAL THINKING

EVALUATING EVIDENCE (MAPS AND ILLUSTRATIONS)

1. Review the chapter (also consult the index to find references in other chapters) to learn the many pursuits of the Beecher children (portrayed on page 309). How do their various contributions reflect the diversity of reform? After conducting this brief biographical inquiry, does the evidence sustain the assertion made about the Beechers at the bottom of page 308?

2. How does the picture entitled *The Constant* on page 316 reflect the ideal of domesticity? What is suggested about the role of a woman in the family? How is it an idealized portrait?

PRIMARY SOURCE: The Role of American Women: Two Views[*]

Catharine Beecher, one of Lyman Beecher's daughters, was one of the leading proponents of the ideal of domesticity in the nineteenth century. She wrote several books defining women's profession in terms of the family and home. In this selection, she discusses women's profession and its relationship to democracy.

> The great maxim, which is the basis of all our civil and political institutions, is, that "all men are created equal," and that they are equally entitled to "life, liberty, and the pursuit of happiness."...But in order that each individual may pursue and secure the highest degree of happiness within his reach...a system of laws must be established, which sustain certain relations and dependencies in social and civil life....There must be the relations of husband and wife, parent and child, teacher and pupil, employer and employed, each involving the relative duties of subordination. The superior in certain particulars is to direct, and the inferior is to yield obedience. Society could never go forward, harmoniously, nor could any craft or profession be successfully pursued, unless these superior and subordinate relations be instituted and sustained....
>
> In this Country, it is established, by both opinion and by practice, that women have an equal interest in all social and civil concerns....But in order to secure her the more firmly in all these privileges, it is decided, that, in the domestic relation, she take a subordinate station, and that, in

---

[*] First excerpt from Catharine E. Beecher, *A Treatise on Domestic Economy* (1841). Second excerpt from *Narrative of Sojourner Truth* (1878). The dialect used by the white reporter, as well as descriptions of the audience's reaction, have been omitted.

civil and political concerns, her interests be intrusted to the other sex, without her taking any part in voting, or in making and administering laws....

It...is in America, alone, that women are raised to an equality with the other sex; and that, both in theory and practice, their interests are regarded as of equal value. They are made subordinate in station, only where a regard to their best interests demands it....In matters pertaining to the education of their children, in the selection and support of a clergyman, in all benevolent enterprises, and in all questions relating to morals or manners, they have a superior influence....

The success of democratic institutions...depends upon the intellectual and moral character of the mass of the people. If they are intelligent and virtuous, democracy is a blessing; but if they are ignorant and wicked, it is only a curse....The formation of the moral and intellectual character of the young is committed mainly to the female hand. The mother writes the character of the future man; the sister bends the fibers that hereafter are the forest tree; the wife sways the heart, whose energies may turn for good or for evil the destinies of a nation. Let the women of a country be made virtuous and intelligent, and the men will certainly be the same. The proper education of a man decides the welfare of an individual; but educate a woman, and the interests of a whole family are secured....

To American women, more than to any others on earth, is committed the exalted privilege of extending over the world those blessed influences, that are to renovate degraded man....The woman who is rearing a family of children; the woman who labors in the schoolroom; the woman who, in her retired chamber, earns, with her needle, the mite to contribute for the intellectual and moral elevation of her country; even the humble domestic, whose example and influence may be moulding and forming young minds, while her faithful services sustain a prosperous domestic state;--each and all may be cheered by the consciousness, that they are agents in accomplishing the greatest work that ever was committed to human responsibility.

Born a slave in New York, Sojourner Truth, then known as Isabella, secured her freedom in 1826. She joined a utopian community and, stirred by religious fervor, adopted her new name and became an itinerant speaker. She embraced abolitionism and eventually the cause of women's rights. Though illiterate, she became a famous orator whose unusual style and deep voice kept audiences spellbound. The following speech was delivered in 1851 at a woman's rights convention in Ohio.

Well, children, where there is so much racket there must be something out of kilter. I think that 'twixt the negroes of the South and the women at the North all talking about rights, the white men will be in a fix pretty soon. But what's all this here talking about? That man over there says that women need to be helped into carriages, and lifted over ditches, and to have the best place every where. Nobody ever helps me into carriages, or over mud puddles, or gives me any best place, and ar'n't I a woman? Look at me! Look at my arm! I have plowed, and planted, and gathered into barns, and no man could head me—and ar'n't I a woman? I could work as much and eat as much as a man (when I could get it), and bear the lash as well—and ar'n't I a woman? I have borne thirteen children and seen them most all sold off into slavery, and when I cried out with a mother's grief, none but Jesus heard—and ar'n't I a woman? Then they talk about this thing in the head—what [is] this they call it? ["Intellect," whispered someone near.] That's it honey. What's that got to do with women's rights or negroes' rights? If my cup won't hold but a pint and yours holds a quart, wouldn't you be mean not to let me have my little half-measure full?

Then that little man in black there, he says women can't have as much rights as man, cause Christ wasn't a woman. Where did your Christ come from?...From God and a woman. Man had nothing to do with him....If the first woman God ever made was strong enough to turn the world upside down, all alone, these together ought to be able to turn it back and get it right side up again, and now they are asking to do it, the men better let them.

Questions

1. Why, according to Beecher, is it proper that in a democracy women have no political rights? Why is the subordination of the wife to the husband necessary in society? Are her arguments convincing?

2. In what ways does Beecher argue that the sexes are equal in America? How is it in women's best interest to be subordinate in some areas? In what areas of life are they superior?

3. How does the style of Sojourner Truth's speech differ from the excerpt by Beecher? What factors contribute to the difference?

4. What is Truth's major point? How does she link the cause of antislavery and women's rights?

5. How do the social backgrounds of both speakers affect their positions?

THE OLD SOUTH

KEYS TO THE CHAPTER

LEARNING OBJECTIVES

When you have finished studying this chapter, you should be able to:

1. Describe the major regions of the South and explain the importance and character of agriculture in the region.

2. Describe the distribution of slavery in the South.

3. Describe the class structure of white southerners and its relationship to slavery.

4. Describe the institution of slavery and how it functioned as a labor system and a system for regulating relations between the races.

5. Describe slave culture and how it helped slaves bear up under the pressures of slavery.

6. Discuss the ways slaves resisted the institution of bondage.

7. Describe the various ways southern whites defended slavery.

THE CHAPTER IN PERSPECTIVE

The religious changes of the Second Great Awakening, the romantic movement, the development of a democratic political culture, and the creation of a domestic national market fundamentally transformed the United States in the years after 1815. These changes were not limited to the North but affected the South as well, in different and dramatic ways. Indeed, as we have seen, it was the rapid expansion of cotton production in the South that propelled the country's explosive economic growth in the 1820s and the 1830s, and slaveholders and slaves had been tied to the international market well before the nineteenth century. The abolition of slavery in the northern states after the Revolution defined southern distinctiveness, as southern values and culture increasingly diverged from the rest of the country. The eclipse of nationalism by southern sectionalism was thus one momentous consequence of the transformations in American life.

OVERVIEW

This chapter examines the values, social structure, and institutions of the Old South—that is, the South before the Civil War. The Old South was a complex society, as four case studies of southern life make clear. White and black southerners, slaveholders, and yeoman farm families lived together in complicated ways. Yet despite the differences, all shared in a characteristic way of life: an agricultural economy resting on the labor of slaves.

The Social Structure of the Cotton South

Cotton was not the only crop grown in the South, but it was the crop that fueled the southern economy and drove both white and slave populations steadily westward and southward. As cotton prices boomed on the world market and the southern Indian tribes were forcibly removed, Southerners poured into the fresh lands of the deep South. A boom mentality gripped Southerners in the Cotton Kingdom, and cotton quickly became the region's major source of wealth. Single-crop agriculture exhausted the soil, plowing accelerated erosion, and deforestation increased epidemic diseases. At the same time, the upper South became more diversified agriculturally, as exhausted soils encouraged a switch to new crops, especially wheat. These crops required less slave labor, hence surplus slaves from the upper South were annually sold to sugar, cotton, and rice planters in the lower South.

The prosperity of southern agriculture helped keep the South overwhelmingly rural. Few cities and towns developed and the South lagged well behind in manufacturing. Schools were rare and southern illiteracy was nearly ten times that of the north.

Slaves and plantations were not found everywhere in the South, but rather where good agricultural land had a ready access to market. Slaves were concentrated along the old eastern seaboard (the Tidewater) and in the new plantation areas of the Deep South. The major source of agricultural labor in the Old South, slavery was a highly profitable investment, making the plantation system possible—which in turn set the tone of Southern culture.

The Class Structure of the White South

At the top of the class structure of the Old South were slaveowners. Only one white southerner in four belonged to a slaveowning family, and fewer than 2 percent were members of the wealthy planter class (20 or more slaves). Most slaveowners owned only a few slaves. The refined plantation society of the Tidewater, with its elegant homes and strong sense of family, was much different from the raw society found on the cotton frontier, where planters often lived in unpretentious homes and an aggressive business outlook was the norm.

Plantations were complex business operations managed by the master. Defenders of slavery stressed the role of paternalism when discussing the relationship between the planter and slaves, but this was more the ideal than reality. Plantation mistresses also had important duties and responsibilities and hardly led lives of leisure. Some complained of their lack of legal rights and especially the sexual relationships between white men and slave women.

The majority of southern whites were non-slaveowning independent yeoman farmers, who owned their own farm and worked it with their family labor. They formed the middle class of the South. Though yeoman farmers were not poor, they were hurt socially and economically by slavery. Nevertheless they supported the institution out of racism and deeply ingrained fears of emancipation. At the bottom of white society were the poor whites, poverty stricken and scorned by other southern whites. Unlike the more prosperous yeoman farmers, the poor whites resented planters, but they disliked blacks even more intensely and were thus strongly opposed to emancipation.

The Peculiar Institution

Most black southerners lived as slaves—part of what was both a labor system and a caste system based on color. They worked long hours and were subject to strict discipline, including physical punishment with a whip. Hardest working were the field hands, organized either by gangs or tasks. Living conditions varied widely, but in general they had a monotonous diet, crude housing, coarse and sometimes inadequate clothing, and limited medical care. As a result, despite population growth, slaves had higher infant mortality and a shorter life expectancy than whites. Slaves resisted the institution in many ways—some overt (like Nat Turner's famous rebellion), most subtle (like destroying or stealing property, or running away). Slavery taught slaves to distrust whites and hide their true feelings in the presence of whites.

Slave Culture

Excluded from white society, slaves developed their own culture that helped them cope with the pressures of bondage. They tried to preserve a sense of family, sang songs that expressed their joy and sorrow as a people, and most important, developed a Christianity of their own that emphasized their dignity as a people and promised them release from the pain of bondage. Slave songs, both spiritual and secular, expressed their innermost feelings, as did folk tales, which in their moral lessons taught young slaves how to survive in a crushing institution like slavery. Slaves were divided by occupations and color, but white racism and the oppression of slavery drove slaves together in a common bond.

Free Southern African-Americans were overwhelmingly located in the upper South. Though a majority lived in rural areas, they were the most urban group in southern society. Few enjoyed economic success. Laws restricting their activities grew more stringent over time. They were trapped in a society that had no place for them.

Southern Society and the Defense of Slavery

As slavery came increasingly under attack, white southerners rallied to defend their "peculiar institution." In 1832, in the aftermath of Nat Turner's rebellion, the Virginia legislature debated the future of slavery, but took no action to end it. Never again would antebellum southerners publicly question slavery. Rather, southern writers developed a series of arguments to defend slavery as a positive good. Southern politicians then felt compelled to defend slavery. In sum, the South had developed a regional identity with some distinct cultural features. But as long as slavery was not a national political issue, the South, with its belief in democracy and white equality and opportunity—and its adherence to Evangelical Protestantism—remained firmly within the American tradition.

KEY EVENTS

1815-1860	*Spread of the cotton kingdom:* cotton becomes the major staple crop in the South
1822	*Denmark Vesey conspiracy:* heightens fears, especially in South Carolina, for the security of slavery
1830-1840	*Proslavery argument developed:* South repudiates antislavery tradition of the Revolution in favor of the view that slavery is a positive good
1830-1860	*Agricultural reform movement in upper South:* restores profitability of agriculture in region
1831	*Nat Turner Rebellion:* precipitates debate over future of slavery in Virginia legislature
1832	*Virginia debate:* legislature declines to take any action against slavery, ending the issue in the South

REVIEW QUESTIONS

MULTIPLE CHOICE

1. "Cotton was king in the Old South." Which statement about cotton is true?
   - a. It was grown primarily in the Upper South.
   - b. It was grown only by the largest slaveowners.
   - c. Cultivation spread steadily westward to new agricultural frontiers.
   - d. In the South, acreage planted in cotton exceeded that devoted to any other single crop.

   (pp. 337-340)

2. Slaveowners made up what proportion of the southern white population?
   - a. 75 percent
   - b. 50 percent
   - c. 25 percent
   - d. less than 2 percent

   (p. 343)

3. For the most part, members of the cotton gentry were:
   - a. self-made men who had succeeded through work and luck.
   - b. the sons of well-to-do Easterners who moved west.
   - c. supported by foreign investors who received most of the cotton revenues.
   - d. members of rich families who used their inheritances to buy plantations.

   (p. 344)

4. In the Old South, plantation mistresses:
   - a. enjoyed lives of leisure with all domestic responsibilities met by slaves.
   - b. bore heavy responsibilities and worked hard to meet them.
   - c. generally lived on the plantations only during the busy social season.
   - d. enjoyed the same legal and social status as their husbands.

   (pp. 345-346)

5. Yeoman farmers in the South:
   - a. were landless and poverty stricken.
   - b. hated the planter class.
   - c. opposed slavery because it hurt them economically.
   - d. suffered from isolation, a limited market, and shortage of money.

   (pp. 347-348)

6. Despite sharp social and economic differences in the Old South, class conflict did not exist because:
   a. there were so few small farmers.
   b. of a shared racism and fear of African-Americans.
   c. even the poorest farmers owned slaves.
   d. planters thought of all white Southerners as social equals.
   (p. 349)

7. A striking feature of American slavery was that:
   a. the slave population increased despite high infant mortality rates.
   b. large numbers of slaves had to be imported to keep the population stable.
   c. the slave population grew at twice the rate of white population growth.
   d. good medical care created a low infant mortality rate among slaves.
   (p. 350)

8. The slave family:
   a. usually consisted of the nuclear unit (father, mother, and their children), but often was part of larger kinship networks.
   b. was essentially impossible to sustain under bondage.
   c. rarely existed in a functional way on large plantations.
   d. by law, had to be sold as a unit.
   (pp. 354-355)

9. Slaves' religion:
   a. was effectively controlled by whites.
   b. was expressed in secret meetings beyond white supervision.
   c. was based primarily on blacks' hatred of whites and thus did not enhance slaves' sense of self-worth.
   d. played only a minor role in the lives of slaves.
   (pp. 356-357)

10. Free blacks in the South:
   a. developed an internal hierarchy favoring darker skin color.
   b. lived mostly in urban centers.
   c. were mostly males.
   d. lived mostly in the upper South.
   (pp. 358-359)

11. All of the following were elements of the proslavery argument developed in the 1830s EXCEPT:

     a. the Bible sanctioned slavery.

     b. southern slaves lived better lives than northern factory workers.

     c. slaves belonged to an inferior race.

     d. slavery, while wrong, was indispensable for the South's economy.

     (pp. 359-360)

12. Nat Turner:

     a. became a leading advocate of slavery as a "positive good."

     b. strongly defended humane treatment of slaves as the slaveowners' paternalistic obligation.

     c. led a slave revolt despite relatively humane treatment by his master.

     d. was an escaped slave who led other runaways to freedom.

     (p. 353)

COMPLETION

Despite its diversity, the South was unified by its rural _____ economy based on _____. _____ was king, but the region's wealth depended on prime agricultural land. The _____ agriculture practiced by southern farmers wore out the soil, and the drive to clear land led to the spread of _____. The _____ diversified its crops, reducing its need for slaves, who were sold to planters in the _____. Most of these slaves worked for a small number of planters. Most whites actually belonged to the _____ class, owning few or no slaves and medium-size farms. The slaves themselves lived in widely varying conditions. Some worked on a _____ system, with constant supervision, while others worked on a _____ system, which allowed them to do what they wished in their extra time. Although slave revolts were uncommon, day-to-day types of _____ occurred more regularly, including work slowdowns and theft. They retained strong _____ ties despite the constant threat of being sold away, and they centered their culture on _____. Over time, slavery became more central to the identity of the South, and politicians even began refining _____ arguments. Even so, Southerners remained strongly tied to the rest of the nation and, before _____, it did not seem inevitable that the two sections would come to blows.

IDENTIFICATION

You should be able to describe the following key terms, concepts, individuals, and places and explain their significance.

Terms and Concepts

Black belt
Cotton kingdom
Poor whites
Virginia debate of 1832

Staple crops
Yeoman farmers
Peculiar institution
Miscegenation

Individuals and Places

Upper South
Deep South
Denmark Vesey

Piedmont
Tidewater
Nat Turner

MAP IDENTIFICATION

On the map, label or shade in the following places. In a sentence, note their significance to the chapter. (For reference, consult the map on page 338 of *Nation of Nations*.)

1. Black belt
2. Deep South
3. Upper South
4. Cotton kingdom
5. Area of rice production
6. Area of sugar production
7. Tidewater
8. Piedmont
9. Mississippi River
10. South Carolina
11. Virginia

South (small)

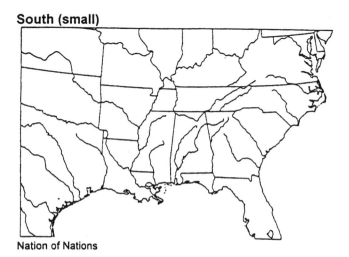

ESSAY

1. Describe the class structure of the Old South. What was the relationship of slaveownership to this class structure?

2. What role did religion play in the lives of slaves? How did that role differ from the role of religion encouraged by many white masters?

3. Describe the change in attitudes toward slavery in the South before and after the early 1830s. What events contributed to that change? What arguments did southerners use to defend slavery?

4. Describe your life as a slave (pick field hand or house servant). What is your average day like? What are the most important things in your life? What is your attitude toward your master and his wife? What do you think you could do as a free black that you can't do as a slave?

5. Do you believe slavery was the most important factor in shaping southern society? If so, explain why, especially since only one-third of southerners were African-American and only one-quarter of southern whites owned slaves or were members of slaveowning families. If you do not believe slavery was the most important factor shaping southern society, what factor was more important?

CRITICAL THINKING

EVALUATING EVIDENCE (MAPS AND ILLUSTRATIONS)

1. Locate the areas of staple crop production (cotton, sugar, rice, tobacco, and hemp) on the map on page 338. Which crop occupies the greatest area? Which is the most geographically specialized? Why are these crops not grown everywhere in the South? What is the relationship of geography to crop production?

2. According to "The Spread of Slavery, 1820-1860" (map, page 341), how did the area of cotton production change between 1820 and 1860? What effect did this have on the distribution of slaves?

3. How does the opening picture (on page 336) illustrate the importance of religion to slaves? Why are the white owner and mistress in the background rather than the center of the scene? What does this picture say about religion and the slave community?

PRIMARY SOURCE: The Break-Up of a Slave Family[*]

Frances A. Kemble was a famous English actress who, on one of her tours of the United States, met and married Pierce Butler, a rice and cotton planter and large slaveholder then living in Philadelphia. A strong opponent of slavery, she accompanied her husband in 1838 to Georgia, where they took up residence. She published an account of her experiences as a plantation mistress, from which this extract concerning her house servant Psyche and her family is taken.

> Early the next morning...I was suddenly startled by hearing voices in loud tones...the noise increasing until there was an absolute cry of despair uttered by some man. I could restrain myself no longer, but opened the door...and saw Joe, the young man, poor Psyche's husband, raving almost in a state of frenzy, and in a voice broken with sobs and almost inarticulate with passion, reiterating his determination never to leave this plantation, never to go to Alabama, never to leave his old father and mother, his poor wife and children, and dashing his hat...upon the ground, he declared he would kill himself if he was compelled to follow Mr. K[ing]. I glanced from the poor wretch to Mr. [Butler], who was standing, leaning against a table with his arms folded, occasionally uttering a few words of counsel to his slave to be quiet and not fret, and not make a fuss about what there was no help for. I retreated immediately from the horrid scene....As soon as I recovered myself I again sought Mr. O—....He then told me that Mr. [Butler], who is highly pleased with Mr. K[ing]'s past administration of his property [as overseer], wished, on his departure for his newly-acquired slave plantation, to give him some token of his satisfaction, and had made him a present of the man Joe, who had just received the intelligence that he was to go down to Alabama with his new owner the next day, leaving father, mother, wife, and children behind....
>
> When I saw Mr. [Butler] after this most wretched story became known to me..., I appealed to him, for his own soul's sake, not to commit so great a cruelty. Poor Joe's agony while remonstrating with his master was hardly greater than mine while arguing with him upon this bitter piece of inhumanity—how I cried, and how I adjured, and how all my sense of justice, and of mercy, and of pity for the poor wretch, and of wretchedness at finding myself implicated in such a state of things, broke in torrents of words from my lips and tears from my eyes!...He gave me no answer whatever, and I have since thought that the intemperate vehemence of my entreaties and expostulations perhaps deserved that

[*] From Frances Anne Kemble, *Journal of a Residence on a Georgian Plantation in 1838-1839* (1863).

he should leave me as he did without one single word of reply; and miserable enough I remained.

Toward evening, as I was sitting alone,...Mr. O— came into the room. I had but one subject in my mind; I had not been able to eat for it. I could hardly sit still for the nervous distress which every thought of these poor people filled me with....I said to him: "Have you seen Joe this afternoon, Mr. O—?"..."Yes, ma'am; he is a great deal happier than he was this morning." "Why, how is that?" asked I, eagerly. "Oh, he is not going to Alabama. Mr. K[ing] heard that he had kicked up a fuss about it" (being in despair at being torn from one's wife and children is called kicking up a fuss; this is a sample of overseer appreciation of human feelings), "and said that if the fellow wasn't willing to go with him, he did not wish to be bothered with any niggers down there who were to be troublesome, so he might stay behind."...

I drew a long breath....The man was for the present safe, and I remained silently pondering his deliverance,...and I think, for the first time, almost a sense of horrible personal responsibility and implication took hold of my mind, and I felt the weight of an unimagined guilt upon my conscience; and yet...when I married...I knew nothing of these dreadful possessions of his, and even if I had I should have been much puzzled to have formed any idea of the state of things in which I now find myself plunged....

Kemble subsequently learned that Butler had purchased Psyche and her children to prevent any separation of the family. She concluded her discussion with the following reflection:

...though [Mr. Butler] had resented my unmeasured upbraidings,...they had not been without some good effect, and though he had, perhaps justly, punished my violent outbreak of indignation about the miserable scene I witnessed by not telling me of his humane purpose, he had bought these poor creatures, and so, I trust, secured them from any such misery....Think...how it fares with slaves on plantations where there is no crazy Englishwoman to weep, and entreat, and implore, and upbraid for them, and no master willing to listen to such appeals.

Questions

1. How are Kemble's antislavery sentiments revealed in her description? What view does her husband take of slavery? Does the reader get any sense of his feelings?

2. Should Kemble have felt any personal responsibility or guilt over the events she describes? Did she fulfill her responsibilities as a mistress in this situation? As a wife? As a woman?

3. What does this account indicate about the relationship between Butler and Kemble? Might this have produced strains in their marriage?

4. Were such occurrences typical in slavery? Is the question of the frequency of the breakup of slave families by sale an important consideration in evaluating slavery?

WESTERN EXPANSION AND
THE RISE OF THE SLAVERY ISSUE

KEYS TO THE CHAPTER

LEARNING OBJECTIVES

When you have finished studying this chapter, you should be able to:

1. Describe the doctrine of Manifest Destiny and how it was used to justify American expansion.

2. Describe the situation in the Mexican borderlands before 1846 and the establishment of the Texas Republic.

3. Describe important features of the Overland Trail experience and of the different societies established in the Far West.

4. Discuss the political origins of the expansion movement, the outbreak of the Mexican War, and the territories added between 1845 and 1848.

5. Explain the rise of the issue of slavery expansion and its relationship to the Mexican War.

6. State the terms of the Compromise of 1850 and its significance.

THE CHAPTER IN PERSPECTIVE

Americans traditionally linked the West with opportunity. The revolutions in markets and transportation greatly accelerated the process of white settlement beyond the Appalachian mountains. Similarly, the spread of cotton production and the quest for economic success had carried Southerners, white and black, free and slave, westward. Thus white southerners linked western expansion with the preservation of not only white opportunity but also slavery. As the lines of settlement spread across the Mississippi River into the Louisiana Purchase, Americans increasingly cast their eyes on neighboring lands to the West that seemed ripe for acquisition. They were also inspired by a long-standing sense of mission, with its vision of the United States as a beacon for the world, and the widespread belief in the impending millennium that fostered so many reform movements in this period. The market revolution (Chapter 10), the new democratic politics (Chapter 11), the energies unleashed by revivalism and reform (Chapter 12), and the expansion of the cotton kingdom

(Chapter 13)—all combined to produce a new expansionist surge in the 1840s. The process that brought Americans into contact with other cultures and peoples forced Americans to confront the slavery issue.

OVERVIEW

This chapter examines the Republic's expansion to the Pacific Ocean, its transformation into a continental nation, and how that development injected the slavery issue into national politics. It begins with the expansion of the Sioux onto the Plains, as a reminder that westward expansion in American history involved more than Anglo-Saxon whites. Moreover, the case of the Sioux illustrates the importance of different kinds of frontiers in the process of expansion. The Sioux conquest of the Plains ultimately depended on the acquisition of guns and horses, and the outbreak of disease epidemics that weakened enemy tribes and shifted the balance of power to the Sioux. Furthermore, Hispanic cultures of the Southwest, as well as the Chinese immigrants of the 1850s, were all a part of the frontier mix.

Destinies: Manifest and Otherwise

In the 1840s, Americans proclaimed that it was the United States' "Manifest Destiny" to expand across the continent. This doctrine combined idealistic impulses—both religious and political—with attitudes of racial superiority and a hunger for good farmland and Pacific trade. Expansion brought Americans into contact—and conflict—with Mexicans in Texas, New Mexico, and California.

Only a few American traders established contact with *rancheros* in California and New Mexico. By contrast, American settlers, initially welcomed by Mexico, poured into Texas, attracted by the promise of free land. They soon became a majority of the population. Tensions with the Mexican authorities led to a revolution. In 1836 Texas forces defeated the Mexican army sent to quell the rebellion, and Texas became an independent republic. Americans in Texas hoped to be annexed to the United States, but the Jackson and Van Buren administrations held back, fearful of stoking the fires of sectionalism.

The Trek West

Lured by the promise of good land and a fresh start, other Americans headed for Oregon and California on the Overland Trail. Most migrants traveled in wagons as part of a family group. The journey, which took six months or more, put heavy pressures on families. Women especially suffered from loss of companionship and their heavy responsibilities on the trail. Forced to perform tasks normally reserved for men, they often saw any semblance of a home, their traditional domain, disappear.

Migration on the overland trail also took a heavy toll on the Plains Indians' way of life. Wagon trains scared off game and used up grass and wood, which prompted the Sioux to demand payment for crossing their lands. Nevertheless, few trains were attacked by Indians.

The Political Origins of Expansion

An odd circumstance made expansion a political issue. The death of the Whigs' first president, William Henry Harrison, brought John Tyler to the presidency. No orthodox Whig, Tyler, a proponent of states' rights, soon broke with the party over economic policy. To garner political support for another term, he took up the Texas issue. The Democratic party countered by dropping Martin Van Buren (who opposed the annexation of Texas) in favor of James K. Polk (who supported it) as the party's presidential candidate. Polk narrowly defeated Henry Clay; Congress responded by annexing Texas.

Polk entered the White House not only supporting Texas annexation but determined to expand American boundaries to acquire the best harbors on the Pacific. He agreed to divide the Oregon territory with Britain, gaining control of Puget Sound. Unable to buy New Mexico and California from Mexico, he provoked war. His belligerence elicited considerable opposition. But the United States quickly conquered New Mexico and California, and when Mexico still stubbornly refused to make peace, American forces occupied Mexico City and forced Mexico to surrender. By the treaty of peace, the U.S. acquired California and New Mexico. But northern Democrats injected the slavery issue into the controversy by introducing the Wilmot Proviso, which sought to ban slavery from any territory gained from Mexico. It never passed, but many northerners by now agreed that slavery—and the political clout of Southerners—must be confined to the South.

New Societies in the West

Overlanders sought to recreate in the West the society they had left behind. With time, these societies became more stable and their economies more diversified. At the same time, as in the East, wealth became more concentrated and opportunity more constricted.

The discovery of gold in California set off a frantic rush to the diggings. The gold rush created a unique society in the mining camps—one that was overwhelmingly male, strongly nativist, transient, and unstable. By 1852 the claims had been worked out and mining was increasingly dominated by heavily capitalized corporations.

Cities also developed in the West. The product of economic self-interest, San Francisco experienced rapid, chaotic growth. It was also an amazingly diverse community ethnically, with large numbers of Europeans, South Americans, Chinese, and other groups. Salt Lake City offered a striking contrast. In order to escape persecution for their unusual beliefs, including polygamy, the Mormons led by Brigham Young moved to the Salt Lake basin. Irrigation enabled them to turn the desert into farmland at the same time it reinforced their sense of hierarchy and unity. A planned community, Salt Lake City had an orderly appearance since its development was carefully regulated by church officials, and the Mormon family was its basic social unit.

By the peace treaty with Mexico, a large number of Hispanics were incorporated into the United States. They came into conflict with the Anglo population, especially in Texas and California. Treated as inferior, harassed, and often reduced to poverty, some expressed their frustration through banditry.

Escape from Crisis

Both major parties tried to avoid the issue of slavery's expansion in 1848. Northern antislavery forces founded a new party, the Free Soil party, which urged adoption of the Wilmot Proviso. In a three-way race, Zachary Taylor, the Whig candidate and a hero of the Mexican War, was elected president. But solution of the territorial question became urgent when California, having quickly gained sufficient population, asked to be admitted as a state.

Congress momentarily settled this question in the Compromise of 1850, devised by Henry Clay and pushed through Congress by Stephen A. Douglas. The compromise admitted California as a free state, included a new fugitive slave law, and adopted the principle of popular sovereignty (the people of the territory should decide) to deal with slavery in the Utah and New Mexico territories.

The Compromise was more an armistice than a compromise, since only one-fifth of the members had supported the entire Compromise. Public opinion in both sections, however, rallied to the compromise measures, and both Whigs and Democrats endorsed the Compromise in their 1852 platforms. An uncontroversial Democrat won the presidency, sectional harmony returned, and it seemed the Union had weathered the sectional storm.

KEY EVENTS

1821	*Mexico wins independence*
1823	*First American settlers in Texas*
1829	*Mexico tries to abolish slavery in Texas:* American slaveholders ignore the law

1830	*Mexico attempts to halt American migration to Texas*
	Joseph Smith founds Mormon Church: despite persecution church recruits many members
1835	*Texas Revolution:* Texas declares its independence
1836	*Santa Anna defeated at San Jacinto:* Mexican control of Texas destroyed, Texas declares itself a republic
1841	*Tyler becomes president:* quickly breaks with Whig party
1844	*Tyler's Texas treaty rejected by the Senate*
	Polk elected president: committed to program of continental expansion
1845	*United States annexes Texas*
1845-1846	*Slidell's unsuccessful mission:* Polk fails to gain additional Mexican territory through negotiations
1846	*War declared against Mexico*
	Oregon treaty ratified
	Wilmot Proviso introduced: injects slavery issue into national politics
1847	*Mormon migration to Utah*
1848	*Treaty of Guadalupe Hidalgo:* U.S. acquires large amount of territory from Mexico
	Free Soil party founded: makes it impossible for major parties to dodge the slavery extension issue
	Taylor elected president: second Whig national victory
1849	*Gold Rush:* California quickly acquires sufficient population for statehood
1850	*Taylor dies and Fillmore becomes president*
	Compromise of 1850 enacted: designed to settle all outstanding sectional differences
1850-1851	*South rejects secession:* southern public opinion accepts the Compromise as a final settlement of sectional crisis
1852	Uncle Tom's Cabin *published*

REVIEW QUESTIONS

MULTIPLE CHOICE

1. The Sioux Indians suffered less from European diseases than did other tribes because:
   a. they had a natural resistance to the diseases.
   b. they were never exposed to European diseases.
   c. their nomadic lives made them less susceptible to epidemics.
   d. they used native plants to limit the extent of epidemics.
   (p. 366)

2. The doctrine of Manifest Destiny:
   a. developed in the 1820s as a popular response to the Monroe Doctrine.
   b. developed as a southern and western reaction to the Panic of 1837.
   c. was used to recruit Americans to migrate to Texas to protect slavery and U.S. interests.
   d. was used to justify U.S. expansion westward in the 1840s.
   (pp. 366-367)

3. All of the following contributed to the growing discontent and eventual revolt of the American settlers in Texas EXCEPT:
   a. the central government's refusal to provide an adequate political participation for settlers.
   b. the government's refusal to provide land for settlers.
   c. a ban on Protestant churches.
   d. a ban on slavery.
   (p. 369)

4. Plains Indians responded to the increasing numbers of emigrants on the Overland Trail by:
   a. demanding compensation from both the government and the emigrants.
   b. refusing to trade with the emigrants.
   c. attacking the wagon trains.
   d. migrating away from the main corridor of travel.
   (pp. 372-373)

5. Texas was finally annexed:
   a. by treaty with Texas when John Tyler first forced the issue.
   b. by joint resolution after the election of 1844.
   c. by joint resolution after Polk became president.
   d. by treaty with Mexico at the end of the Mexican War.
   (p. 374)

6. Under President James K. Polk, the United States:
    a. purchased the Oregon Territory from Great Britain.
    b. went to war with England to gain the Oregon Territory.
    c. reached a compromise with the British over the Oregon Territory.
    d. delayed dealing with the British over the Oregon question until the war with Mexico was over.
    (p. 374)

7. The Mexican War began when:
    a. the United States annexed Texas.
    b. the Bear Flag revolt broke out in California.
    c. American and Mexican troops clashed in the disputed territory.
    d. Taylor crossed the Nueces River and occupied Mexico City.
    (p. 375)

8. The Wilmot Proviso:
    a. was an attempt to prohibit slavery from any territory acquired from Mexico.
    b. condemned Polk for starting the Mexican war.
    c. voted supplies for American troops but opposed acquiring any territory.
    d. stipulated Mexicans in the ceded territories would have rights of American citizenship.
    (p. 377)

9. Brigham Young led his followers west in 1847:
    a. in order to fulfill biblical prophecy.
    b. as the result of a split with other church leaders.
    c. because government officials had ordered him to be arrested.
    d. to escape persecution and interference with the church.
    (p. 383)

10. John C. Calhoun argued that:
    a. popular sovereignty should decide slavery's status in the territories.
    b. slavery was legal in all the territories.
    c. slavery could never exist in the territory acquired from Mexico.
    d. slavery should be prohibited from all the territories.
    (pp. 384-385)

11. The Compromise of 1850 included all these provisions EXCEPT:
    a. the Wilmot Proviso.
    b. a new fugitive slave law.
    c. organization of the Utah and New Mexico territories.
    d. establishment of a Texas-New Mexico boundary.
    (pp. 386-387)

12. In the early 1850s:
   a. most Southerners rejected the Compromise of 1850.
   b. most Northerners rejected the Compromise, but most Southerners supported it.
   c. the Whig and Democratic parties both repudiated the Compromise in the 1852 election.
   d. Americans generally supported the Compromise of 1850.
   (p. 388)

COMPLETION

During the 1840s, the concept of _____ became commonly accepted, as the United States acquired nearly 1.5 million square miles of new territory. Much of this land had previously been under the control of _____ and then _____, which gained its independence in 1821. At first Mexico encouraged American immigration to Texas, but in _____ led a military expedition into the territory to force Americans to abide by _____ law. A rebel contingent led by _____ defeated the Mexicans and Texas declared itself _____. During this same period, Americans traveled the _____ to establish new settlements in Oregon. There were many dangers on the journey, but the threat of the _____ was generally exaggerated. The new president, _____, elected primarily because of his pro-expansion policies, was faced with potential conflicts with two foreign powers. He settled the dispute over Oregon with _____ and maneuvered the troops of General _____ in the hopes of starting a fight with Mexico. His efforts succeeded and the _____ was won with a relatively small cost in American lives. The war caused the _____ issue to reemerge as the nation decided how to assimilate its new territories. The first conflict arose over the _____, which tried to bar slavery from the new territories. Tensions rose higher as a new political party called the _____ made restriction of slavery its primary issue. Finally, _____ was able to broker the Compromise of _____, which temporarily eased tensions.

IDENTIFICATION

You should be able to describe the following key terms, concepts, individuals, and places and explain their significance.

Terms and Concepts

Manifest Destiny
Mormon Church
Popular sovereignty
Treaty of Guadalupe Hidalgo
Wilmot Proviso
Ranchero
Fugitive slave law
Nashville convention
Gold rush

Bear Flag Rebellion
Texas Revolution
Compromise of 1850
Oregon Treaty
Slave Power
Omnibus bill
Uncle Tom's Cabin
Secession
Polygamy

Individuals and Places

James K. Polk
William Henry Harrison
Zachary Taylor
James G. Birney
Brigham Young
Oregon Trail
Santa Anna
Nueces River
Millard Fillmore
John L. O'Sullivan

John Tyler
Henry Clay
John C. Calhoun
Martin Van Buren
Texas Republic
Stephen Austin
Sam Houston
Stephen A. Douglas
Great Salt Lake basin
Rio Grande boundary

MAP IDENTIFICATION

On the map on the following page, label or shade in the following places. In a sentence, note their significance to the chapter. (For reference, consult the maps in *Nation of Nations* on pages 375 and 386.)

1. Nueces River
2. Rio Grande
3. 36° 30' line
4. Utah Territory
5. New Mexico Territory
6. California
7. Oregon Territory

Nation of Nations

8. 49th parallel
9. Original boundary of Texas (when a Mexican province)

West

ESSAY

1. You are traveling the Oregon Trail. Write journal entries describing your experiences and how they are the same or different from those your spouse is experiencing.

2. Congress had to decide how to deal with the issue of slavery in the territory it acquired after the Mexican War. Describe the four options proposed for dealing with the issue.

3. List the provisions of the Compromise of 1850. Which provisions favored the North? Which ones favored the South?

4. Name at least three events that contributed to the rise of the slavery issue in American politics in the 1840s. Why did each one have this effect?

5. What are alternative ways to focus on the frontier besides the westward movement of whites? Discuss the experiences of the Sioux, the Chinese, and the Mexican residents of the borderlands in answering the question.

6. Describe the doctrine of Manifest Destiny. Why did it arise in the 1840s?

CRITICAL THINKING

EVALUATING EVIDENCE (MAPS AND ILLUSTRATIONS)

1. On the map on page 365, in which direction did the gun frontier move? Which direction did the horse frontier move? When did they intersect?

2. Why did the Overland Trail follow rivers (page 371)? Locate the major mountain passes the trail crossed. Where did the trail divide into a California and an Oregon branch? Why there and not earlier or later? Why is the last third of the route the most difficult?

3. What territories were subject to popular sovereignty (page 386)? What territories were free? What proportion of all territories was open to slavery? Why did Southerners feel they had gotten less than their share of new territory? What was the relationship of the Mexican Cession (page 365) and "unorganized territory" to the Missouri Compromise line of 36° 30'?

4. What aspects of San Francisco's early growth are illustrated in the picture on page 380? How does it portray the city's population? Why are there so few women and children in the picture?

PRIMARY SOURCE: An American View of Mexican California[*]

A member of a prominent Massachusetts family, Richard Henry Dana Jr. dropped out of Harvard University in 1834 because of poor health and signed on as a common sailor "before the mast." He sailed around Cape Horn to California, where he and his shipmates collected cattle hides destined for the shoe factories of Lynn. These excerpts are from an account based on the notes and diary he kept while a sailor.

> *The Californians are an idle, thriftless people, and can make nothing for themselves. The country abounds in grapes, yet they buy bad wine*

---

[*] From Richard Henry Dana Jr., *Two Years Before the Mast* (1840).

Nation of Nations

made in Boston and brought round by us, at an immense price, and retail it among themselves at a real [a Spanish coin then worth 12½ cents] by the small wine-glass....[They] buy shoes (as like as not, made of their own hides, which have been carried twice round Cape Horn) at three and four dollars, and "chicken-skin" boots at fifteen dollars apiece. Things sell, on an average, at an advance of nearly three hundred per cent upon the Boston prices....

Their complexions are various, depending—as well as their dress and manner—upon their rank; or, in other words, upon the amount of Spanish blood they can lay claim to. Those who are of pure Spanish blood, having never intermarried with the aborigines, have clear brunette complexions, and sometimes, even as fair as those of English women. There are but few of these families in California....These form the aristocracy; intermarrying, and keeping up an exclusive system in every respect. They can be told by their complexions, dress, manner, and also by their speech....From this upper class, they go down by regular shades, growing more and more dark and muddy, until you come to the pure Indian, who runs about with nothing upon him but a small piece of cloth, kept up by a wide leather strap drawn round his waist. Generally speaking, each person's caste is decided by the quality of the blood, which shows itself, too plainly to be concealed, at first sight. Yet the least drop of Spanish blood...is sufficient to raise them from the rank of slaves, and entitle them...to call themselves Españolos, and to hold property, if they can get any....

Another thing that surprised me was the quantity of silver that was in circulation....The truth is, they have no credit system, no banks, and no way of investing money but in cattle. They have no circulating medium but silver and hides—which the sailors call "California bank notes." Everything that they buy they must pay for in one or the other of these things....

No Protestant has any civil rights, nor can he hold any property, or, indeed, remain more than a few weeks on shore, unless he belongs to some vessel. Consequently, the Americans and English who intend to reside here become Catholics, to a man; the current phrase among them being,— "A man must leave his conscience at Cape Horn."...

The government of the country is an arbitrary democracy; having no common law, and no judiciary. Their only laws are made and unmade at the caprice of the legislature, and are as variable as the legislature itself....Revolutions are matters of constant occurrence in California.

They are got up by men who are at the foot of the ladder and in desperate circumstances, just as a new political party is started by such men in our own country. The only object, of course, is the loaves and fishes; and instead of caucusing, paragraphing, libelling, feasting, promising, and lying, as with us, they take muskets and bayonets, seizing upon the presidio and custom-house, divide the spoils, and declare a new dynasty. As for justice, they know no law but will and fear....

Such are the people who inhabit a country embracing four or five hundred miles of sea-coast, with several good harbors; with fine forests in the north; the waters filled with fish, and the plains covered with thousands of herds of cattle; blessed with a climate, than which there can be no better in the world; free from all manner of diseases...; and with a soil which corn yields from seventy to eighty fold. In the hands of an enterprising people, what a country this might be! we are ready to say. Yet how long would a people remain so, in such a country? The Americans (as those from the United States are called) and Englishmen, who are fast filling up the principal towns, and getting the trade into their hands, are indeed more industrious and effective than the Spaniards; yet their children are brought up Spaniards, in every respect, and if the "California fever" (laziness) spares the first generation, it always attacks the second.

Questions

1. What qualities does Dana ascribe to the Mexican residents of California? Is his description critical? Does he note any positive qualities of Californians?

2. By what standards does he judge the Californians? How do Dana's observations reflect his cultural background? How would his comments reinforce the assumptions of his readers?

3. What kind of society does Dana describe? How does it differ from American society?

4. What is his view of the government? How is it different from that in the United States? What role does race play in California's society? Is this different from the situation in the United States?

5. How are Dana's values as revealed in this selection similar to the attitudes associated with Manifest Destiny that are described in the text? How could a proponent of American expansion find in his description justification for the United States taking over California?

THE UNION BROKEN

KEYS TO THE CHAPTER

LEARNING OBJECTIVES

When you have finished studying this chapter, you should be able to:

1. Describe the changes in the economy in the 1850s and indicate how they contributed to the sectional conflict.

2. Discuss the impact of immigration on American society and politics in this period.

3. Trace how and why the second party system collapsed, to be replaced by a sectional alignment.

4. Discuss the rise of the Republican party to national power.

5. Describe the events during Buchanan's administration and indicate how they heightened the sectional conflict.

6. Give the reasons for southern secession and the outbreak of war.

THE CHAPTER IN PERSPECTIVE

The Compromise of 1850 proved to be an armistice rather than a settlement of the sectional crisis. The issues raised by America's geographic expansion in the 1840s, particularly the status of slavery in the territories, burst forth again in the 1850s to shatter the Union. Several earlier developments contributed to the intensifying sectional conflict in this period. The revivals of the Second Great Awakening and the abolitionist movement which began in the 1830s had a continuing impact. So did the evolution of the democratic political system, with its tendency to appeal to popular emotions. The unique features of the culture of the Old South, which largely derived from the institution of slavery, fostered fears among southern whites for their security and the security of slavery in the Union. And finally, the expansion of the market and the national transportation system had an uneven impact on the sections and weakened the economic and political alliance between the West and the South.

OVERVIEW

Popular sovereignty seemed to be the only means of compromise over the question of slavery in the Western territories. That idea failed dismally in Kansas, as was dramatically highlighted by an 1856 raid on Lawrence, Kansas, by a proslavery band, and John Brown's retaliatory Pottawattomie massacre. The escalating violence during the decade, most visibly in Kansas, pointed grimly to the impending breakup of the union.

Sectional Changes in American Society

The coming of the war occurred against the backdrop of continuing economic transformation that widened the gulf between northern and southern societies. Railroad construction became the dominant influence on economic growth. Railroads opened new lands to settlement, which in turn added more areas to the wider market. Railroads and high grain prices in Europe stimulated the expansion of commercial agriculture in the North, making grain exports as crucial to the nation's economy as cotton exports. The railroad network also served to link the West economically to the East rather than the South. Railroads altered the prairie landscape, and ambitious farmers plowed up the native grasses and planted wheat and other commercial crops. At the same time, industry boomed in the North and an immense tide of immigrants (especially Irish, Germans, and Scandinavians) provided cheap labor for the factories and swelled northern population (and thus political power) at the expense of the South.

With cotton prices relatively high, the South prospered in the 1850s. Even so, southern leaders complained about their section's dependence on the North for manufactured goods, shipping, and marketing services. Efforts to promote industrialization in the South or diversify its economy failed. The rising cost of slaves also reduced planters' margin of profit.

The Political Realignment of the 1850s

The fragile political system collapsed when Congress, spurred by Illinois Senator Stephen Douglas, passed the Kansas-Nebraska Act, repealing the Missouri Compromise of 1820 and opening the remaining regions of the Louisiana Purchase to slavery under the doctrine of popular sovereignty. Thus the slavery issue was placed again at the center of national politics. At the same time, native-born Americans voiced growing hostility to the influx of immigrants. Given these strains, the old Jacksonian party system crumbled.

First to benefit from this political chaos was the secret nativist Know-Nothing or "American" party, which called for restrictions on the political power of immigrants and Catholics. The party grew rapidly in 1854 and 1855; so many Whigs joined the Know-Nothings that the Whig party folded. But at the height of its power, the Know-Nothing organization itself split over sectional issues and disappeared.

Meanwhile, northerners and southerners raced to settle Kansas. The first elections in the territory were marred by massive proslavery fraud, and before long, fighting broke out between proslavery and antislavery partisans. The continuing turmoil in Kansas, coupled with a brutal attack on Senator Charles Sumner of Massachusetts in the Senate Chamber in May 1856, greatly strengthened a new sectional party, the Republicans. By the 1856 election the Republicans had emerged as the strongest party in the North and the second strongest party in the nation, after the Democrats. The Republican party stood for the ideal of free labor. On ideological and moral grounds, they opposed the expansion of slavery and argued that the aristocratic Slave Power threatened republican government and the rights of white northerners.

The Worsening Crisis

Despite the Republicans' strong and unexpected showing, the Democrats carried the 1856 election. James Buchanan, the Democratic candidate, took office in 1857 intending to dampen sectional fury. These hopes were ruined by the Supreme Court's *Dred Scott* decision, which held that Congress could not prohibit slavery from a territory. Since this was their principal demand, Republicans were outraged. But Douglas' popular sovereignty was called into question as well. And Buchanan's effectiveness was further weakened by the beginning of a depression in 1857, which hurt the North more than the South.

Buchanan's attempt to force the admission of Kansas through Congress under the proslavery Lecompton Constitution split the Democratic party along sectional lines. Douglas broke with the president on this issue, marshaling opposition in Congress, which ultimately rejected the Lecompton Constitution. But Douglas was now the symbol of the deep sectional divisions in the Democratic party. In 1858 Abraham Lincoln challenged Douglas in Illinois for his Senate seat. Douglas narrowly won re-election, but Lincoln's strong race brought him national recognition and stature.

Southerners increasingly fretted about the future. They feared the growing power of what they called the "Black Republicans." They feared that white opportunity was eroding and that without new lands, slavery and the southern economy would stagnate. Various proposals to relieve the South's internal crisis failed, and more and more southern whites felt morally and politically isolated.

The Road to War

John Brown's attack on Harpers Ferry in 1859 further alarmed southerners. They were even more shocked at the support Brown received from some prominent northern intellectuals. Such suspicions strengthened disunion sentiment. The Democratic party split in 1860, each faction nominating its own presidential candidate. The result was a four-way contest, in which Abraham Lincoln, the Republican candidate, won the presidency on the strength of northern electoral votes, earning less than 40 percent of the popular vote nationwide. For the first time, a sectional antislavery party had elected a president.

Following Lincoln's election, the seven states of the Deep South, led by South Carolina, seceded and organized the Confederate States of America. Congress defeated all proposals to resolve the crisis; compromise efforts were doomed since neither the Republicans nor the secessionists of the Deep South were willing to make any concessions. When Lincoln sent supplies to the Union garrison at Fort Sumter, Confederate batteries opened fire and captured the fort. The North rallied to Lincoln's call for troops to restore the Union, but four more southern states—the upper South—seceded. The diverging economies of the two sections, the acute issue of slavery's status in the West, the weaknesses of the nation's political system, the ideology of republicanism with its fears of conspiracies against liberty, the differences between slave and free societies—all were crucial to this outcome. And the war came.

KEY EVENTS

1840-1860   *Expansion of railroad network:* western trade reoriented toward the East

1846-1854   *Mass immigration to United States:* nativist feeling intensifies

1854   *Kansas-Nebraska Act:* repeal of Missouri Compromise produces great northern outcry

Republican party organized: sectional party tries to capitalize on anti-Nebraska sentiment in the North

Peak of immigration: Know-Nothings rapidly gain popularity

1855   *Fighting begins in Kansas:* increases sectional tensions

Republican party organizes in key northern states: but makes little headway against the Know-Nothings

1856	*Sack of Lawrence:* strengthens the Republican party
	Caning of Charles Sumner: incident strengthens the Republican party
	Pottawattomie massacre: violence escalates in Kansas as a result of John Brown's murders
	Buchanan elected president: Democrats narrowly beat back the Republican challenge
1857	*Dred Scott decision:* ruling that Congress cannot prohibit slavery from a territory creates a political furor
	Panic and depression: Democrats weakened
	Lecompton Constitution drafted: recognizes the legality of slavery in Kansas
1858	*Congress rejects Lecompton Constitution*
	Lincoln-Douglas debates: establish Lincoln as a national Republican leader
1859	*John Brown's raid on Harpers Ferry:* southern fears, disunion sentiments intensify
1860	*Democratic party ruptures at Charleston:* party divides along sectional lines
	Lincoln elected president: first national triumph of a sectional antislavery party
	South Carolina secedes
1861	*Rest of Deep South secedes; Confederate States of America established*
	Crittenden Compromise defeated: hopes for peaceful settlement dashed
	War begins at Fort Sumter: Confederacy resists Lincoln's effort to resupply the fort

REVIEW QUESTIONS

MULTIPLE CHOICE

1. Beginning in 1840, the driving force in the American economy was:
    a. cotton production.
    b. gold and silver mining.
    c. railroad construction.
    d. the production of high-grade steel.
    (p. 393)

2. In the South during the 1850s:
    a. the falling price of cotton created a recession that impoverished many.
    b. advocates of a "New South" established large textile factories.
    c. investment in land and slaves precluded capital investment in manufacturing.
    d. Southerners advocated national policies to support economic development.
    (p. 399)

3. The Kansas-Nebraska Act:
    a. ensured that the number of free and slave states would remain equal.
    b. repealed the Missouri Compromise and authorized the residents of both territories to determine the status of slavery.
    c. temporarily suspended the Missouri Compromise until the Kansas Territory determined the status of slavery.
    d. created the slave territory of Kansas and the free territory of Nebraska.
    (p. 400)

4. The Republican party advocated all the following ideas EXCEPT:
    a. slavery would drive free labor out of the territories.
    b. the Slave Power was determined to destroy the liberties of Northerners.
    c. slavery was morally wrong.
    d. popular sovereignty was the best way to handle the question of slavery expansion.
    (pp. 402-406)

5. The Dred Scott decision:
    a. declared Congress could not prohibit slavery from a territory.
    b. struck down the Kansas-Nebraska Act.
    c. endorsed the Wilmot Proviso.
    d. upheld the Missouri Compromise.
    (pp. 406-407)

6. The Lecompton constitution:
   a. allowed Kansans to vote on whether they wanted slavery.
   b. represented a majority of the legitimate residents of Kansas.
   c. tried to make Kansas a free state.
   d. was the work of a proslavery minority in Kansas.
   (pp. 407-408)

7. John Brown's raid at Harpers Ferry:
   a. was endorsed by the Republican party.
   b. precipitated a slave insurrection.
   c. was ignored by Southerners because of its small size.
   d. strengthened disunion sentiment in the South.
   (p. 411)

8. All of the following were candidates for president in 1860 EXCEPT:
   a. James Buchanan.
   b. John C. Breckenridge.
   c. Stephen A. Douglas.
   d. Abraham Lincoln.
   (pp. 412-413)

9. Abraham Lincoln:
   a. won an overwhelming popular and electoral victory in 1860.
   b. was elected with only a bare majority of the popular and electoral vote.
   c. won the presidency with less than 40 percent of the popular vote.
   d. was elected to the presidency by the House of Representatives.
   (p. 413)

10. Which was NOT part of the Crittenden Compromise?
    a. establishment of the Missouri Compromise line.
    b. an amendment protecting slavery in the states.
    c. the admission of Kansas as a slave state.
    d. a congressional slave code to protect slavery in the territories.
    (pp. 413-414)

11. In his first inaugural address, President Lincoln:
    a. announced the withdrawal of all Federal personnel from the South as a gesture of good will.
    b. declared that a state of war existed between the United States and the Confederacy.
    c. promised to abolish slavery no matter what the consequences.
    d. promised not to abolish slavery but vowed to preserve the Union.
    (pp. 414-415)

12. All of the following helped cause the Civil War EXCEPT:
    a. inherent weaknesses in the American political system.
    b. the economic independence of each section of the nation.
    c. diverging economies in the North and the South.
    d. Americans' conspiratorial view of politics.
    (pp. 415-416)

COMPLETION

The struggles in "Bleeding _____" in the 1850s indicated serious tensions between North and South. A proslavery raid on _____ was followed by the massacre at _____, led by _____. The differences between the _____ went beyond efforts of ineffective politicians and an unwillingness to compromise. Development of the national network of _____ left the Old Northwest more closely linked with the East. Southerners complained that the North used its control over _____ to convert the South into a colony. The development of a national transportation network further inflamed the slavery issue, as Senator _____ introduced the Kansas-Nebraska Act, in part because he hoped development of these territories would further the chances of Chicago becoming the eastern terminus of the transcontinental railroad to California. The Kansas-Nebraska Act repealed the _____ and introduced the concept of _____ in its place. This led to the battles in Kansas and the caning of _____ on the Senate floor. The new _____ Party's credibility was enhanced by this incident because its claims about the threat posed by the _____ to northern civil liberties now seemed credible. The next event to inflame sectional differences was the _____ decision, which declared that Congress had no power to ban slavery from any of the territories. John Brown's raid on the federal armory at _____ shocked the South. They were convinced that the raid was engineered by the Republican Party, and when the Republican nominee for president, _____ was elected in _____, the movement toward _____ began.

IDENTIFICATION

You should be able to describe the following key terms, concepts, individuals, and places and explain their significance.

Terms and Concepts

Popular sovereignty
Dred Scott decision
Congressional slave code
Know-Nothing party
Lecompton Constitution
Slave Power
Sack of Lawrence
Crittenden compromise
Pottawatomie massacre
Lincoln-Douglas debates

Secession
Freeport doctrine
Kansas-Nebraska Act
Bleeding Kansas
Bleeding Sumner
Constitutional Union Party
Uncle Tom's Cabin
Panic of 1857
Confederate States of America

Individuals and Places

John Brown
Abraham Lincoln
John C. Breckinridge
Roger B. Taney
Franklin Pierce
Preston S. Brooks
Harriet Beecher Stowe
Harpers Ferry

Stephen A. Douglas
James Buchanan
John Bell
Fort Sumter
Charles Sumner
Jefferson Davis
John C. Frémont
John J. Crittenden

MAP IDENTIFICATION

On the map, label or shade in the following places. In a sentence, note their significance to the chapter. (For reference, consult the map in *Nation of Nations* on page 414.)

1. South Carolina
2. States that seceded before Lincoln's inauguration
3. States that seceded after the firing on Fort Sumter
4. Slave states that did not secede

South with clear state borders

ESSAY

1. List four major sectional events of the period from 1854 to 1856. Which of these events aided the Republican party?

2. What did the Supreme Court rule in the *Dred Scott* decision? Why did the decision fail to settle the slavery expansion issue?

3. "Ever since the Revolution, when Americans accused the king and Parliament of deliberately plotting to deprive them of their liberties, Americans were on the watch for political conspiracies." Give examples of the way in which (a) northerners feared that the Slave Power was conspiring against them and (b) southerners, beleaguered and anxious, worried about the plots of the "Black Republicans."

4. Give yourself an occupation, a geographic location, and a political affiliation. Which side did you take once secession began? Why? Which of the following factors do you feel was most central in provoking civil war: the debate over slavery, the debate over states' rights, the growing economic and social differences between North and South, differing ideological commitments to republicanism by Northerners and Southerners, the failures of political leaders. Defend your position by discussing specific events from the 1850s.

CRITICAL THINKING

EVALUATING EVIDENCE (MAPS AND ILLUSTRATIONS)

1. Where did most railroad construction in the 1850s occur (map, page 394)? Why did the main lines run east-west rather than north-south?

2. What territory was open to slavery after passage of the Kansas-Nebraska Act (map, page 401)? How much territory did that law affect?

3. Locate the 36° 30' line on the Kansas-Nebraska Act map on page 401. How many slave states were north of this line? Do you think there would have been a good chance for slavery to thrive in Kansas?

4. According to the map on secession, page 414, which five states had the highest proportion of white families owning slaves? How many of these seceded before Lincoln took office? Which five southern states had the lowest proportion of white families owning slaves? How many of these states seceded? Evaluate the relationship between the extent of slave ownership and the strength of secession sentiment in the South.

6. How does the picture for the play of *Uncle Tom's Cabin* (page 405) try to enlist the sympathies of the viewer? What symbols are used to condemn slavery?

7. Photography was hardly a decade old when the portraits of Douglas and Lincoln (page 409) were taken. Suggest how and why the photograph would quickly be added to the arsenal of campaign weapons in the age of democratic politics.

PRIMARY SOURCE: The South Reacts to Lincoln's Election

The following editorials from southern newspapers during the secession crisis discuss southern complaints and grievances following Lincoln's election. Neither the *Bee* nor the *Crescent*, both of which urged moderation during the 1860 presidential campaign, had been in the vanguard of the secession movement. Lincoln's election revolutionized public opinion in the Deep South, however, and both papers quickly endorsed secession.

> They [Northerners] know that the South is the main prop and support of the Federal system. They know that it is Southern productions that constitute the surplus wealth of the nation, and enables us to import so largely from foreign countries. They know that it is their import trade that draws from the people's pockets sixty or seventy millions of dollars per annum, in the shape of duties, to be expended mainly in the North, and in the protection and encouragement of Northern interests. They know that it is the export of Southern productions, and the corresponding

import of foreign goods, that gives profitable employment to their shipping. They know that the bulk of the duties is paid by the Southern people, though first collected at the North, and that, by the iniquitous operation of the Federal Government, these duties are mainly expended among the Northern people. They know that they can plunder and pillage the South, as long as they are in the same Union with us, by other means, such as fishing bounties, navigation laws, robberies of the public lands, and every other possible mode of injustice and peculation. They know that in the Union they can steal Southern property in slaves, without risking civil war, which would be certain to occur if such a thing were done from the independent South....

These are the reasons why these people do not wish the South to secede from the Union. They are enraged at the prospect of being despoiled of the rich feast upon which they have so long fed and fattened, and which they were just getting ready to enjoy with still greater...gusto.

—From the New Orleans *Daily Crescent*, January 21, 1861

Another error...is the belief that the South has been moved to resistance chiefly by the adverse result of the Presidential contest. We are told with marked emphasis that Lincoln has been elected in strict conformity to the mandates of the Constitution and the provisions of the law. Now this is not denied, nor does the South profess to desire a separation exclusively or even chiefly on account of the success of the Black Republican nominee. That was but the crowning stroke to a protracted and wanton series of aggressions on the South;...the final and fitting upshot to a long-continued policy of injustice and oppression. Lincoln's triumph is simply the practical manifestation of the popular dogma in the free States that slavery is a crime in the sight of GOD, to be reprobated by all honest citizens, and to be warred against by the combined moral influence and political power of the Government. The South, in the eyes of the North, is degraded and unworthy, because of the institution of servitude. She is hated by the North because she holds the black race in bondage. She is persecuted because fanatics have made unto themselves a peculiar code of ethics with which the South does not agree, because she knows it to be fallacious.

It is self-evident that if one-half of the people of a country look upon the other half as in the perpetual commission of a heinous offense before GOD, and disseminate the doctrine that they are guilty of the grossest violation of civil, social and religious canons, the section deemed thus culpable must be regarded as inferior in every respect to the former....If

Nation of Nations

this is a sentiment compatible with the endurance of a Union avowedly founded on the most perfect political equality and social harmony and fraternity, then we must ignore the history of our revolutionary struggles, our efforts in behalf of a sound government, and our success in the formation of the Constitution of the United States.

—From the New Orleans *Bee*, December 10, 1860

Questions

1. What economic questions are emphasized in these editorials? Are these legitimate grievances?

2. Were economic issues critical to the origins of the Civil War?

3. Why did Southerners fear the Republican party? Why did they refer to it as the Black Republican party?

4. What specific events in the 1850s support each of these assertions of northern aggression: "They have robbed us of our property,…they have set at naught the decrees of the Supreme Court, they have invaded our States and killed our citizens, they have declared their unalterable determination to exclude us altogether from the Territories, they have nullified the laws of Congress?"

5. What importance do these editorials place on the issue of slavery? Was slavery the most important cause of southern secession?

6. How would a northern Republican respond to the accusations and grievances contained in these editorials?

TOTAL WAR AND THE REPUBLIC

KEYS TO THE CHAPTER

LEARNING OBJECTIVES

When you have finished studying this chapter, you should be able to:

1. Discuss the concept of total war and its relevance to the Civil War.

2. Assess the leadership of Abraham Lincoln and Jefferson Davis, and describe the strategies and military campaigns each pursued.

3. Discuss Lincoln's decision to make emancipation a war aim, the significance of the Emancipation Proclamation, and the eventual passage of the Thirteenth Amendment.

4. Describe the meaning and impact of the war for civilians, African-Americans, and women.

5. Describe the experiences of the soldiers in both armies.

6. Evaluate the reasons for the Confederacy's defeat.

THE CHAPTER IN PERSPECTIVE

The Civil War grew out of major differences dividing the North and the South. Slavery was at the heart of these differences, yet the North went to war claiming that its sole purpose was to preserve the Union and the Confederacy insisted it was fighting for independence, not slavery. The ideals and arguments of both sides drew upon the American past. Supporters of the Union denied, as Jackson had denied in his proclamation on nullification, that there was any right of secession. Supporters of the Union upheld the idea of America's mission going back to the Revolution. Confederates argued, as had Calhoun in the nullification crisis, that a state had the right to secede under the Constitution. In establishing the Confederacy, Southerners declared that they acted on the principle of self-government, as proclaimed by the Revolution's leaders in resisting tyranny in 1776. Yet ironically, it was a future in the making, not a mythical past reclaimed, that was at stake. The war would unleash forces that impelled both sides to adopt new ideas and principles; in the process, the meaning of the Civil War and the character of American society were to be fundamentally transformed.

OVERVIEW

The Civil War was the first total war in history, a war that depended on the mobilization of a society's human, economic, and intellectual resources. Before the first major battle, at Bull Run, neither side had anticipated the magnitude of the struggle ahead. The northern defeat at Bull Run forced members of Congress and other leaders to recognize that victory would not come easily or quickly. It would require total war, and it would transform society.

The Demands of Total War

At the outset, the North seemed to have overwhelming economic and military advantages. But the South, fighting for a cause on its own soil, had counterbalancing advantages. The North would have to rely on better technology—and better leadership. The war's two political leaders were a study in contrasts. While hardworking, the Confederate President, Jefferson Davis, was a less effective leader than the Union's Abraham Lincoln. Lincoln ably persuaded northerners of American ideals. He also recognized the need to follow a strategy of isolation and invading the South. Concerned about the border states, Lincoln moved aggressively to hold them for the Union. In the process, a new border state, West Virginia, comprising counties with strong Unionist support, was admitted to the Union.

Opening Moves

The Union began a blockade of the southern coast and beefed up naval strength on the rivers. In addition, European powers refused to recognize the Confederacy or intervene militarily. The first Union combat successes occurred in the West, where Ulysses S. Grant invaded Tennessee. His drive south stalled after the fierce battle of Shiloh. In the East, the leading Union commander was George McClellan, whose well-drilled army was much larger than his opponent's but whose ingrained caution prevented him from using it aggressively. In Virginia, a stalemate quickly developed, as Robert E. Lee defeated a series of Union invasions yet was stalled himself at Antietam when he invaded Maryland. After a year and a half of hard fighting with heavy losses on both sides, no end to the war was in sight.

Emancipation

As the fighting dragged on, Lincoln—whose announced priority was to save the Union—came under mounting pressure to attack slavery as a way to win the war. Congress passed a series of laws that undermined slavery, and the Union refused to return runaway slaves to their owners. Believing that slavery should be abolished by state action, Lincoln at first tried to get the border states to adopt gradual emancipation. Rebuffed, he decided to act against slavery himself. Following the battle of Antietam, he announced a preliminary Emancipation Proclamation; the final Proclamation took effect on January 1, 1863, freeing the slaves in all areas under Confederate control. The war, as Europeans recognized, had been redefined into a crusade to revolutionize the nation.

A large number of slaves, perhaps as many as half a million, eventually fled to the Union lines and were freed. Many of these freed slaves were put to work at minimal wages on plantations in Union-controlled areas of the Mississippi Valley. Even those who remained in the Confederacy challenged white authority. The Union also accepted African-Americans into the army and navy. Most were former slaves. As soldiers, African-Americans impressed white comrades with their courage and fierce fighting.

The Confederate Home Front

War fundamentally transformed southern society. It brought increasing hardship and moral decay. With European exports severely cut by the blockade, the Confederacy attempted to build up its industry in order to become self-sufficient. With so many men mobilized into the army, it fell to women to run the farms and supply the necessary labor in factories. But inflation and food shortages became worse each year.

In an effort to win the war, Davis and his advisers concentrated power in the government at Richmond, provoking strong protests from many southerners who had gone to war to preserve states' rights. The draft—first in American history—was especially denounced. With tax revenues insufficient to finance the war, the Confederate population suffered from rampant inflation. Bread riots broke out in several cities. The moral tone of society plummeted, as gambling, drinking, speculation, and crime overran the South.

The Union Home Front

Civilians in the North suffered less. As it mobilized its economic resources, the Union prospered. Congress financed the war's costs through a combination of the first federal income tax, borrowing, and printing "greenbacks." These revenues were then spent on war materials. The economy boomed, but fraud plagued government purchases and workers saw their real wages decline. A speculative fever pervaded society, and Washington, D.C., no less than Richmond, sank in a swamp of moral decadence.

As in the South, women ran farms and took factory jobs to maintain war production. They soon came to dominate the formerly male professions of nursing and teaching. Much of the volunteer work in the Union to provide relief and medical supplies was done by women.

Lincoln cracked down on antiwar activities by suspending the writ of habeas corpus, an action that was quite controversial. He also authorized military trials of civilians, an action the Supreme Court declared illegal after the war. The draft, which allowed the wealthy to hire a substitute or pay 300 dollars for an exemption, also illustrated the expanded power of the federal government. Peace Democrats, labeled Copperheads by Republicans, vigorously protested the government's violations of personal liberty, and a major anti-draft riot erupted in New York City in 1863.

Gone to be a Soldier

Soldiers in both armies—mostly young, mostly farmers—soon discovered that war was much more tedious and far less glamorous than they had envisioned. Soldiers experienced great hardship from disease, poor food, and exposure, as well as risking life and limb in fighting. Traditional moral standards declined under the pressures of war. Paradoxically, both armies experienced religious revivals. Accustomed to the freedom of the farm, southern soldiers did not adjust as easily to military discipline, and southern individualism eventually weakened the army, especially as the Union war effort became increasingly organized. Most significantly, combat had become far more deadly than ever before. New technology, particularly the rifled musket and anti-personnel artillery, caused much higher numbers of battle casualties, as the defense became considerably stronger than the offense.

The Union's Triumph

The war's turning point came in 1863 when the Union won concurrent victories at Gettysburg and Vicksburg. Gettysburg destroyed Lee's offensive capabilities, while Grant's victories in the west that year led Lincoln to appoint him commanding general. With the Mississippi in Union hands, Grant instructed William Tecumseh Sherman to drive a diagonal wedge through the Confederacy from Tennessee through Georgia, while Grant himself fought a series of fierce battles with Lee in Virginia.

Grant was unable to break Lee's lines and, with Sherman bogged down in front of Atlanta, Lincoln seemed headed for defeat in the 1864 presidential election. Sherman's capture of Atlanta in September was the military breakthrough Lincoln needed, and he swept to victory. Lincoln's re-election made it clear that the Union would continue the war until reunion and abolition of slavery were achieved. Following the election, Congress approved the Thirteenth Amendment abolishing slavery; it was ratified by December 1865.

With the Confederacy's hopes flickering, Jefferson Davis offered to abolish slavery in a desperate and unsuccessful bid for British recognition. In the meantime, Sherman embarked on his destructive march through Georgia and then the Carolinas. Civilian morale collapsed in the Confederacy. In April, Grant forced Lee to surrender at Appomattox Court House. The rest of the Confederate armies soon did the same. But in the hour of Union victory, Lincoln was assassinated, the final tragedy in the conflict.

The Impact of War

The war profoundly changed the nation, altering its political institutions, its economy, and its values. Battle deaths nearly equaled the loss of life from all other wars combined. Secession was dead, and power was concentrated in the federal government. Slavery had been abolished, the South's wealth and political power destroyed. Industry was stimulated and, with the probusiness Republican party dominant, the government now played a much more active role in the economy. But the war had a high spiritual cost: sectional bitterness, a greater tolerance of corruption, moral complacency, and a loss of the crusading idealism that had characterized the nation before the war.

KEY EVENTS

1861

Border states remain in the Union: major strategic victory for the Union

Lincoln suspends writ of habeas corpus in selected areas: war infringes on civil liberties

Battle of Bull Run: illusion of short war destroyed

Crittenden Resolution: Congress declares that the war is being fought solely to preserve the Union

1862

Battle of Shiloh: Grant's drive South checked with heavy losses indicating the magnitude of this conflict

Slavery abolished in the District of Columbia

Confederacy institutes draft: growing complaints against interference with individual liberty

Homestead Act: to promote rapid settlement of the West

Union Pacific Railroad chartered

Land Grant College Act: sale of specified public lands to be used to promote higher education

Second Confiscation Act: slaves of rebel masters declared free if in Union custody

Union income tax enacted: federal government assumes new powers

McClellan's Peninsula campaign fails: hopes for decisive victory in East dashed

Battle of Antietam: Lee's invasion of Maryland turned back

Lincoln suspends writ of habeas corpus throughout Union: more sweeping interference with civil liberties

Battle of Fredericksburg: Union morale reaches lowest point

1863

Emancipation Proclamation: Lincoln declares slaves in Confederacy free

National Banking Act: Congress brings currency, most banks under a central national system

Union institutes draft: resentment in the Union because of special privileges

Bread riots in the Confederacy: taxes, high prices, and inflation lead to disorder

West Virginia admitted to the Union

Battle of Gettysburg: Lee's invasion of the North repulsed, destroying his army's offensive capability

Vicksburg captured: Union in control of the Mississippi River, dividing the Confederacy

New York City draft riots: resentment against draft sparks a bloody anti-black, anti-Republican riot

1864

Grant becomes Union general-in-chief: Union war effort given a new aggressiveness

Wilderness Campaign: Grant hammers at Lee's lines with horrendous losses

Fall of Atlanta: Sherman's victory gives Lincoln a needed boost

Lincoln reelected: makes reunion and emancipation certain

Sherman's march to the sea: stunning demonstration of psychological warfare against civilians

1865

Lee surrenders: Confederate resistance quickly collapses

Lincoln assassinated

Thirteenth Amendment ratified: slavery abolished in the United States

REVIEW QUESTIONS

MULTIPLE CHOICE

1. At the beginning of the Civil War, which one of the following factors favored the Confederacy?

    a. the transportation system.
    b. the manpower pool.
    c. the fact that the fighting would be on southern soil.
    d. the South's existing industrial capacity.
    (pp. 420-421)

2. The Confederacy hoped to gain European recognition because:
   a. it had slavery.
   b. it repudiated the Monroe Doctrine.
   c. cotton was vital to England's economy.
   d. the Confederacy was a military threat to Europe.
   (pp. 424-425)

3. The battle at Antietam was significant for all the following reasons EXCEPT:
   a. it demonstrated McClellan had the qualities necessary to win the war.
   b. it provided the occasion for Lincoln to announce the preliminary Emancipation Proclamation.
   c. it repulsed a Confederate invasion of the North.
   d. it was the bloodiest one-day battle in the history of American warfare.
   (pp. 427, 430)

4. The Crittenden Resolution:
   a. called for negotiations with the Confederacy to end the war.
   b. proclaimed runaway slaves to be contraband.
   c. declared that the war was being fought to free the slaves.
   d. declared that the war was being fought to save the Union.
   (p. 429)

5. The Emancipation Proclamation applied to slaves:
   a. in those areas of the South under Union control.
   b. in those areas of the South under Confederate control.
   c. in all the southern states.
   d. of masters who were disloyal.
   (p. 430)

6. During the Civil War, African-American troops:
   a. were not allowed to see combat duty.
   b. suffered casualty rates just slightly lower than white troops.
   c. served in segregated units under the command of white officers.
   d. were integrated into units in the Regular Army.
   (pp. 430-432)

7. During the war, women did all the following EXCEPT:
   a. enter the professions of nursing and teaching.
   b. take jobs in the government bureaucracy.
   c. run the farms and plantations.
   d. run the railroads.
   (pp. 433, 436-437)

8. The Republican Congress during the Civil War passed economic legislation that included all EXCEPT:

     a. a system of nationally chartered banks.

     b. restricting money to hard currency ("specie").

     c. an increase in tariff duties.

     d. the country's first income tax.

     (pp. 435-436)

9. Lincoln suspended the writ of habeas corpus:

     a. only in the border states.

     b. throughout the North.

     c. for all crimes committed during the war.

     d. from the beginning of the war until September 1862.

     (p. 438)

10. The Confederacy was like the North in each of the following ways EXCEPT:

     a. each president, despite little military background, ably directed the war effort.

     b. each government relied initially on volunteer soldiers, but later had to institute a draft that provoked deep hostility.

     c. each government financed the war through taxes and issuing paper money.

     d. the demands of war increased the power of the central government and accelerated industrialization on both sides of the Mason-Dixon line.

     (throughout chapter)

11. During the Civil War:

     a. about one-third of the casualties occurred because of diseases.

     b. twice as many troops died from diseases than from battle wounds.

     c. military discipline ensured that the soldiers enjoyed good health.

     d. Union troops suffered few disease-related deaths.

     (p. 440)

12. The surrender of Robert E. Lee:

     a. brought an almost immediate end to all fighting in the Civil War.

     b. resulted in his arrest and a 25-year prison term for treason.

     c. meant the capture of the last major Confederate army.

     d. did not end the fighting in Tennessee.

     (p. 448)

Nation of Nations

COMPLETION

Most northerners believed the _____ would be defeated quickly. The _____ held the advantage in manpower and _____ capacity. The _____ enjoyed strategic advantages because it did not have to _____ the North to win, only defend its own _____. Almost no one was prepared for the kind of _____ war that occurred, with its enormous casualties and the need for enormous contributions from the _____ populations. The South won the first military battle at _____; the North had already won its first victory by keeping the _____ in the Union. This showed the superior _____ skills of Abraham Lincoln in comparison with the Confederate president, _____. The biggest problem _____ had was his inability to find an effective commanding general. _____ fought Lee to a stalemate at _____ but had what Lincoln called a "case of the slows." The Confederate army had a brilliant leader in _____. Another problem Lincoln had was defining the _____ of the North. By 1863 he decided to issue the _____, which freed all slaves in areas controlled by the Confederacy. 1863 was also the year the war turned militarily, with the North's victories at both _____ and _____. Lincoln finally settled on _____ as his commanding general and Northern armies began making significant inroads into the South. General _____ made his famous _____ in 1864, capturing Atlanta and inflicting devastating damage on the southern countryside. General Lee surrendered at _____, but only five days later Lincoln was _____ at Ford's theater.

IDENTIFICATION

You should be able to describe the following key terms, concepts, individuals, and places and explain their significance.

Terms and Concepts

Writ of habeas corpus
Copperhead
Thirteenth Amendment
First Confiscation Act
Border states
Crittenden Resolution
Ex parte Milligan

March to the sea
Conscription
Emancipation Proclamation
Contraband
Radical Republicans
Second Confiscation Act
King Cotton diplomacy

Individuals and Places

Bull Run

Gettysburg

Antietam

Abraham Lincoln

Ulysses S. Grant

William Tecumseh Sherman

Alexander H. Stephens

Thomas "Stonewall" Jackson

Appomattox

Chancellorsville

Vicksburg

Shiloh

Jefferson Davis

Robert E. Lee

George McClellan

Joseph Johnston

West Virginia

David Farragut

MAP IDENTIFICATION

On the map on the following page, label or shade in the following places. In a sentence, note their significance to the chapter. (For reference, consult the maps in *Nation of Nations* on pages 426, 428, 443, and 445.)

1. Shiloh
2. New Orleans
3. Vicksburg
4. Mobile
5. Atlanta
6. Savannah
7. Sherman's march to the sea
8. Gettysburg
9. Bull Run
10. Antietam
11. Richmond
12. Washington, D.C.

ESSAY

1. Discuss how four of the following factors worked as an advantage for either North or South: geography, political leadership, military leadership, manpower, industrial capacity, relative strength of the central government, a "cause" to fight for.

2. You are Abraham Lincoln. Why did you hesitate at first to make emancipation a goal of the war and then why did you change your mind? What policies toward emancipation did you eventually pursue?

3. What does the idea of total war mean? Give at least three ways that the Civil War was a total war. What was the significance of each factor you have listed? Which one was the most important, in your view?

South with borders and rivers

4. What advantages did the Confederacy have when the war began? How did the Union overcome these advantages?

5. What was the impact of the war on the home front in the Union and the Confederacy?

6. List four ways the war changed the nation. What is the significance of each point you note?

CRITICAL THINKING

EVALUATING EVIDENCE (MAPS AND ILLUSTRATIONS)

1. Looking at the map, "The War in the East, 1861-1862" (page 428), how did the proximity of Washington to Richmond determine the area of fighting in the eastern theater?

2. Why did the opening fighting in the West occur in the Mississippi Valley (map, page 426)? Where were the initial Union gains in territory? Why do you suppose eastern Tennessee, which was strongly Unionist, was more difficult to occupy?

3. Looking at the map, "The War in the West, 1861-1862" (page 426), what was the importance of Union control of the Mississippi River?

4. What was the basic Union strategy in the western theater from 1863-1865? Why were Tennessee and Georgia, and not Alabama or the interior of Mississippi, the scene of Union operations? What was the significance of Sherman's march through Georgia?

5. Of the categories listed in the table on page 421, which one gave the Union the greatest proportional advantage? Of those categories in which it had an advantage, for which was its proportional advantage lowest?

6. Of the items included in the table on page 421, which one do you think had the greatest bearing on the outcome of the war? Why?

7. Most of the Union's railroad track mileage was in the North, far from the area of fighting. Why then was this a military advantage?

8. As the table on page 421 indicates, in aggregate tonnage the Union's advantage in shipping stemmed from the merchant marine rather than the navy. Why was this a military advantage for the Union? Why did the lack of shipping tonnage hurt the Confederacy militarily?

PRIMARY SOURCE: The Gettysburg Address and Lincoln's Second Inaugural[*]

Abraham Lincoln delivered this brief address at the dedication of the cemetery at Gettysburg on November 19, 1863. Contrary to the popular myth that he casually wrote out the talk on the back of an envelope, Lincoln carefully crafted his remarks before leaving Washington and continued to work on them on the way to Gettysburg. This is the final text.

> Four score and seven years ago our fathers brought forth on this continent, a new nation, conceived in Liberty, and dedicated to the proposition that all men are created equal.
>
> Now we are engaged in a great civil war, testing whether that nation, or any nation so conceived and so dedicated, can long endure. We are met on a great battle-field of that war. We have come to dedicate a portion of that field, as a final resting place for those who here gave their lives that the nation might live. It is altogether fitting and proper that we should do this.

---

[*] From Roy P. Basler, ed., *The Collected Works of Abraham Lincoln.*

But, in a larger sense, we can not dedicate—we can not consecrate—we can not hallow—this ground. The brave men, living and dead, who struggled here, have consecrated it, far above our poor power to add or detract. The world will little note, nor long remember what we say here, but it can never forget what they did here. It is for us the living, rather, to be dedicated here to the unfinished work which they who fought here have thus far so nobly advanced. It is rather for us to be here dedicated to the great task remaining before us—that from these honored dead we take increased devotion to that cause for which they gave the last full measure of devotion—that we here highly resolve that these dead shall not have died in vain—that this nation, under God, shall have a new birth of freedom—and that government of the people, by the people, for the people, shall not perish from the earth.

Lincoln delivered his second inaugural address on March 4, 1865. With the war only a few weeks from conclusion, and the Union flushed with the anticipation of victory, he took the occasion to reflect on the meaning of the terrible conflict, the role of slavery in the war's origins, and God's judgment on the nation. Lincoln's brief speech is notable for its humility in the hour of victory, for its magnanimity toward a defeated foe, and for its vision of peace and sectional harmony. Along with the Gettysburg Address, it is the supreme statement of the meaning and purpose of America's greatest war.

On the occasion corresponding to this four years ago, all thoughts were anxiously directed to an impending civil-war. All dreaded it—all sought to avert it....Both parties deprecated war; but one of them would make war rather than let the nation survive; and the other would accept war rather than let it perish. And the war came.

One eighth of the whole population were colored slaves, not distributed generally over the Union, but localized in the Southern part of it. These slaves constituted a peculiar and powerful interest. All knew that this interest was, somehow, the cause of the war. To strengthen, perpetuate, and extend this interest was the object for which the insurgents would rend the Union, even by war; while the government claimed no right to do more than to restrict the territorial enlargement of it. Neither party expected for the war, the magnitude; or the duration, which it has already attained. Neither anticipated that the cause of the conflict might cease with, or even before, the conflict itself should cease. Each looked for an easier triumph, and a result less fundamental and astounding. Both read the same Bible, and pray to the same God; and each invokes His aid against the other....The prayers of both could not be answered; that of neither has been answered fully. The Almighty has His own purposes....If we shall suppose that American Slavery is one of those offences which, in the providence of God, must needs come, but which, having continued through His appointed time, He now wills to remove, and that He gives to both North and South, this terrible war, as the woe due to those by whom the offence came, shall we discern therein any departure from those divine attributes which the believers in a Living God always ascribe to Him? Fondly do we hope—fervently do we pray—that this mighty scourge of war may speedily pass away. Yet, if God wills that it continue, until all the wealth piled by the bond-man's two hundred and fifty years of unrequited toil shall be sunk, and until every drop of blood drawn with the lash, shall be paid by another drawn with the sword, as was said three thousand years ago, so still it must be said "the judgments of the Lord, are true and righteous altogether."

With malice toward none; with charity for all; with firmness in the right, as God gives us to see the right, let us strive on to finish the work we are in; to bind up the nation's wounds; to care for him who shall have borne the battle, and for his widow, and his orphan--to do all which may achieve and cherish a just, and a lasting peace, among ourselves, and with all nations.

Questions

1. What meaning does Lincoln give to the war in the Gettysburg Address? Does he attach the same meaning to the conflict in the Second Inaugural?

2. When does Lincoln date the birth of the United States? Why did he select this date?

3. What does Lincoln mean by "a new birth of freedom?" Is the claim that Lincoln makes no reference to slavery in this speech correct?

4. How does Lincoln place the war in the United States in a larger setting? What significance does it have for the rest of humankind?

5. In the Second Inaugural, what does Lincoln say was the relationship between slavery and the war?

6. What does Lincoln mean in the Second Inaugural when he says each side looked for "a result less fundamental and astounding?"

7. What concerns do you think Lincoln had about the war's impact on this nation? What were his hopes once peace was restored? How would the type of peace described by Lincoln mitigate the war's tragedy?

RECONSTRUCTING THE UNION

KEYS TO THE CHAPTER

LEARNING OBJECTIVES

When you have finished studying this chapter, you should be able to:

1. Discuss the twofold challenge of Reconstruction following the defeat of the Confederacy.

2. Describe Lincoln's and Johnson's plans of Reconstruction, and the failure of Johnson's program.

3. Describe the growing conflict between Johnson and Congress over Reconstruction.

4. Discuss the nature of Congressional Reconstruction, including the principal laws and amendments passed as part of this program.

5. Discuss the course of Reconstruction in the southern states, including the aspirations and experiences of black southerners.

6. Describe the abandonment of Reconstruction, the causes for its failure, and its racial legacy.

THE CHAPTER IN PERSPECTIVE

The Civil War resolved several long-standing problems in the Republic. For one, the threat of secession had been laid to rest; the Union was perpetual, as Andrew Jackson had proclaimed in 1832. Slavery had also been destroyed, and with it the most "peculiar" feature of the culture of the Old South. With the agrarian South vanquished and impoverished, the industrial North was now the dominant section politically and economically, and the nation's course toward full industrialization was established. But the war had also created new problems. What rights the former slaves would have, and what their place would be in American society, was unclear. Similarly, how the former states of the Confederacy would regain their rights was uncertain. These two interrelated issues constituted the "problem of Reconstruction."

Yet if the potential for far-reaching change existed at the end of the war, key elements of the American political tradition exerted a restraining influence. For example, although the federal government exercised greater power after the war than before, most Americans believed that protecting individual rights was the responsibility of the states. In addition, the fear of a standing army remained undiminished. Not only had the Union army been quickly demobilized, but Northerners were uncomfortable at the thought of a prolonged military occupation of the South or the active intervention of the army in domestic affairs. Finally, bolstered by the market revolution, Americans remained wedded to the doctrines of private property, self-reliance, and individual achievement, values that worked against any program of government assistance to the freed slaves. It was within this mix of change and tradition—of the possibility to overthrow the past and the desire to conserve it—that Reconstruction would take shape and eventually unravel.

OVERVIEW

Shortly after the war, Benjamin Montgomery, an extraordinary ex-slave, purchased the plantation of Confederate president Jefferson Davis. Through energy and hard work, Montgomery became a leading planter in the postwar South during the period of Reconstruction, when the South was in the process of resuming its place in the Union. Montgomery's hopes and aspirations symbolized both the possibilities for significant change in the South and the ultimate challenge of Reconstruction. Would the newly freed slaves gain economic opportunity—and the political power needed to secure it? More broadly, how would victorious North and vanquished South readjust their economic and political relations?

Presidential Reconstruction

Even during the war, Lincoln formulated plans for the restoration of the Union once the fighting was over. Lincoln favored a generous peace, since he was eager to bring states back into the Union and wanted to build up a Republican party in the South by attracting former Whigs. Radical Republicans in Congress, concerned about protecting the rights of former slaves and convinced that Congress should control re-admission, found Lincoln's plan too lenient. Lincoln vetoed a Radical plan in 1864, but by war's end he seemed to be moving in the direction of the Radicals.

Lincoln's assassination elevated Andrew Johnson, a War Democrat from Tennessee, to the presidency. Johnson moved in the summer of 1865 to implement a program less stringent even than Lincoln's original plan. Under Johnson's guidelines, all the former states of the Confederacy established new state governments in 1865. Yet southern whites refused to give blacks any political rights, instead passing a series of black codes, laws designed to keep blacks an uneducated, propertyless, agricultural laboring class. In addition, white southerners defiantly elected prominent former Confederates to office.

Congressional Radicals strongly disagreed with Johnson over securing the place of African-Americans in American society. Congress repudiated Johnson's program in December 1865, refusing to seat representatives from the former Confederate states. Moderate Republicans, who favored protecting black rights if not remaking southern society (as the Radical minority wanted), were driven by presidential vetoes into an alliance with the Radicals. Together they extended the life of the Freedmen's Bureau over Johnson's veto in order to provide assistance to former slaves and passed the Fourteenth Amendment. This amendment made blacks citizens, and extended basic civil rights to all citizens. indirectly opening the possibility for black male suffrage. Tennessee ratified the amendment, and was promptly readmitted to the Union. The remaining ten states of the old Confederacy refused and remained under military rule. Johnson took his case against Congress to the northern people in the fall elections of 1866. To his dismay, Republicans won a sweeping victory; with two-thirds majorities in both houses of Congress, they could now override any presidential veto.

Congressional Reconstruction

Given a popular mandate, Republicans in Congress proceeded to enact their own program of Reconstruction, requiring the unreconstructed states to ratify the Fourteenth Amendment and adopt black suffrage. States that delayed the process were forced to do so. Congress refused, however, to redistribute land to freed slaves, believing that giving blacks the ballot was sufficient.

Johnson tried to obstruct the Congressional program by interpreting laws as narrowly as possible. When the president attempted to remove Secretary of War Edwin Stanton, a Radical, in defiance of the new Tenure of Office Act, the House finally impeached Johnson. He was acquitted in the Senate by one vote. Those who voted for acquittal were uneasy about using the impeachment process to resolve a political dispute between the two branches of government.

Reconstruction in the South

Under Congress' program, radical governments, representing new Republican coalitions, assumed power in the South. None was controlled by black southerners, though blacks did serve. Ranging widely in ability, black officeholders generally came from the top rungs of African-American society.

In most southern states, black voters did not form a majority. Republicans needed white support as well. Native white southerners who joined the party were branded scalawags; they were often Unionists from the hill counties or former Whigs attracted by the party's economic nationalism. Northerners who came South after the war and held public office were derisively referred to as carpetbaggers. Contrary to their image, they were not all poor and self-interested. Less swayed by racial feelings than were southern-born white Republicans, they disproportionately held the highest offices in the Republican regimes.

The new southern state constitutions adopted some important reforms, most notably the establishment of public schools, and granted black suffrage. But they were cautious on the issue of social equality and did not forbid segregation.

The southern Republican governments confronted the problem of rebuilding the war-ravaged South. They sought to encourage industrialization and expand the railroad network. Taxes went up with expenditures, and these governments came under heavy attack for corruption. Corruption certainly existed—indeed, it was a nationwide problem—but opponents exaggerated its extent for partisan purposes. In truth, the major objection of opponents to these governments was that they shared power with blacks.

Black Aspirations

Initially, black southerners thought of freedom largely as a contrast to slavery: the freedom to move about to work where they wished, to be free from physical punishment and the breakup of families. In freedom, blacks moved to strengthen their families, pursue education, and establish their own churches. They negotiated new working conditions with white landlords, refusing to live in the old slave quarters or work in gangs under the supervision of an overseer. Eventually the system of sharecropping evolved as the way to organize black agricultural labor—a higher status arrangement but harshly exploitative. The Freedmen's Bureau supervised the contracts between white landlords and black workers, and special Freedmen's Courts adjudicated disputes. The Bureau's record in protecting blacks varied considerably, but in general it had only limited success, due largely to the fact that Congress let it expire.

Planters responded to emancipation by seeking physical and psychological separation from former slaves. They discarded the old paternalist ideal in favor of segregation. Less prosperous than before the war, they developed a new way of life based on segregation and sharecropping.

The Abandonment of Reconstruction

In 1868 the Republicans successfully nominated Ulysses S. Grant for president. Grant would come to symbolize a waning of the zeal to enforce and maintain Reconstruction. Republicans tried to make Reconstruction more secure by passing the Fifteenth Amendment, which forbade a state from denying the right to vote on grounds of race, though women's suffrage advocates regretted that discrimination based on gender was not included.

Grant lacked the skill or moral commitment to make Reconstruction succeed. Scandals rocked his administration, creating widespread popular disenchantment and fostering the Liberal Republican revolt in 1872. As charges of corruption swelled and disorder continued unabated in the South, northern public opinion, which never had much faith in the abilities of former slaves, became increasingly disillusioned with Reconstruction. In addition, the beginning of a severe depression in 1874 directed public attention closer to home and gave Democrats control of the House for the first time since 1861.

With the northern commitment weakening, white southerners stepped up their assault on the radical governments in the South. They used social ostracism, economic pressure, and racist appeals to undermine Republican support. Their most effective weapon, however, was terror and violence directed against Republican leaders and black voters. The constant violence in the South during elections further weakened the northern commitment to Reconstruction.

In the end, this combination of southern white terror and northern white weariness—and a political deal—combined to end Reconstruction. The 1876 presidential election failed to produce a clear winner. A special electoral commission by a straight party vote declared Republican Rutherford B. Hayes the winner. To secure their victory, in private negotiations Republicans had agreed to restore home rule in the South in exchange for Hayes' election. This deal became known as the Compromise of 1877. Once in office, Hayes dutifully withdrew support for the remaining radical governments in the South and they collapsed. Every southern state had been "redeemed" by 1877; Reconstruction was at an end. The antebellum reform impulse had eroded, and a new materialism turned attention from protecting black rights. Republicans split over tactics: Blacks themselves lacked education and experience. By both weakening northern resolve and stimulating southern white resistance, racism played a major role in the failure of Reconstruction. One isolated symbol of this failure came in 1878, when Benjamin Montgomery lost his land—to Jefferson Davis.

KEY EVENTS

1863   *Lincoln outlines Reconstruction program:* moves to establish loyal governments

1864   *Lincoln vetoes Wade-Davis bill:* Radicals bitterly denounce the president

Louisiana, Arkansas, and Tennessee establish governments under Lincoln's plan: none grant suffrage to blacks

1865   *Freedmen's Bureau established*

Johnson becomes president: puts his program of Reconstruction in place in the summer of 1865

Congress excludes representatives of Johnson's governments

Thirteenth Amendment ratified: slavery abolished

Joint Committee on Reconstruction established: Congress demands say in shaping Reconstruction policy

1865-1866   *Black codes enacted:* southern states limit rights of former slaves

1866   *Civil Rights bill passed over Johnson's veto*

Memphis and New Orleans riots: anti-black and anti-Republican violence alarms northern public opinion

Tennessee readmitted to Congress: first Confederate state to regain representation

Republicans victorious in congressional elections: northern voters repudiate Johnson and his program

1867   *Congressional Reconstruction*

Tenure of Office Act: Congress tries to prevent Johnson from removing Secretary of War Edwin Stanton

Ku Klux Klan organized: southern white resistance to Reconstruction turns to violence

1867-1868   *Constitutional conventions in the South:* new, progressive state constitutions adopted

African-Americans vote in southern elections

1868	*Johnson impeached but acquitted:* Radical power peaks
	Fourteenth Amendment ratified: Congress seems to protect black rights, impose black suffrage only in southern states
	Grant elected president: Republicans shocked at closeness of the election
1869	*Fifteenth Amendment passes Congress:* Republicans seek to make black suffrage constitutionally secure
1870	*Last southern states readmitted to Congress:* remaining states required to ratify both the Fourteenth and the Fifteenth Amendment
1871	*Ku Klux Klan Act:* government moves to break up the Ku Klux Klan
1872	*General Amnesty Act:* all but a handful of prominent Confederate leaders pardoned
	Freedmen's Bureau dismantled
1873-1877	*Panic and depression:* Republican party hurt by hard times
1874	*Democrats win control of the House*
1875	*Civil Rights Act:* Congress seeks to protect black rights
1876	*Disputed Hayes-Tilden election*
1877	*Compromise of 1877:* Hayes declared winner of electoral vote, last Republican governments in South fall

REVIEW QUESTIONS

MULTIPLE CHOICE

1. Abraham Lincoln's plan of reconstruction required:

     a. 50 percent of the adult white males to take the loyalty oath.

     b. 10 percent of the adult white males to take the loyalty oath.

     c. the abolition of slavery with compensation.

     d. blacks be given the right to vote.

     (p. 455)

2. Under the new president Andrew Johnson, presidential reconstruction:
      a. would implement a harsh program in the South.
      b. adhered substantially to the views of Congressional leaders.
      c. made it possible for former high-ranking Confederates to assume positions of power in the reconstructed southern governments.
      d. never was implemented because Congress passed its own program before Johnson's could go into effect.
      (pp. 456-457)

3. In May 1868:
      a. Andrew Johnson became the first president to be removed from office.
      b. Andrew Johnson resigned from the presidency rather than face certain impeachment and removal.
      c. the House of Representatives refused to approve articles of impeachment.
      d. the Senate failed by one vote to convict Andrew Johnson of the impeachment charges filed against him.
      (pp. 462-463)

4. The African-Americans elected to political offices during Reconstruction:
      a. were more conservative than the majority of the black population.
      b. overwhelmingly advocated land reform as crucial to true freedom.
      c. briefly dominated all of the state governments of the former Confederacy.
      d. tended to be poor, uneducated, and unqualified to hold elective offices.
      (p. 463)

5. The most important institutions for African-Americans as they tried to establish their own independent family and community life were:
      a. the Freedmen's Bureau and the Supreme Court.
      b. the black-controlled state legislatures and the land reform program.
      c. the sharecropping system and the black codes.
      d. the schools and the churches.
      (pp. 465-469)

6. In the years after the Civil War, most freedpeople ended up working:
      a. as farmers on land they owned.
      b. as farmers under a sharecropping system.
      c. as wage laborers in the new textile mills.
      d. as itinerant day laborers in domestic and service jobs.
      (pp. 468-469)

7. The Freedmen's Bureau courts:
    a. consistently sided with the planters.
    b. consistently sided with the freedmen.
    c. were the most effective means of protecting black economic rights.
    d. were declared unconstitutional by the federal courts.
    (pp. 469)

8. The Fifteenth Amendment:
    a. prohibited denying the right to vote on grounds of race.
    b. enacted women's suffrage.
    c. forbid literacy tests or property requirements for voting.
    d. imposed black suffrage only in the South.
    (p. 471)

9. The Civil Rights Act of 1875:
    a. eliminated social segregation in the North and in the South.
    b. never passed Congress despite pressure from President Grant.
    c. was vetoed by President Ulysses Grant and never went into effect.
    d. contained provisions for social equality that were later declared unconstitutional.
    (p. 472)

10. The primary purpose of the Ku Klux Klan was to:
    a. keep former slaves from finding jobs.
    b. force all African-Americans to leave the South.
    c. help Republican candidates win elections in Southern states.
    d. destroy the Republican party in the South.
    (p. 473)

11. The Compromise of 1877:
    a. provided for a recount of votes in the former Confederate states.
    b. underscored Republican resolve to continue Reconstruction.
    c. gave the presidency to Tilden.
    d. marked the end of Reconstruction.
    (p. 474)

12. Reconstruction ended:
    a. despite strong northern sentiments to continue Radical policies.
    b. without any positive results for African-Americans or the nation.
    c. in failure because of deep-seated racism in the United States.
    d. as a success because northern blacks had gained social equality.
    (pp. 475-476)

COMPLETION

With the war over, Republican leaders began the process of _____ the Union. Lincoln had hoped to attract former southern Whigs into the Republican Party by providing a _____ peace. However, the _____ Republicans who took over after Lincoln's death were more concerned with the rights of the _____ than with conciliating the South. They clashed with _____, who was a supporter of states' rights and a tactless politician. In 1866, they passed a civil rights bill over the President's _____. The bill was designed to overturn the more flagrant provisions of the _____, which intended to keep African-Americans propertyless laborers with inferior legal rights. When Johnson vetoed bills and tried to have Radicals removed from the cabinet, the House of Representatives voted articles of _____. During this conflict Republican moderates constructed the most lasting legacies of Reconstruction, the _____ Amendments, which protected individual rights from the power of state governments and prohibited the denial of voting rights based on race, color, or previous condition of servitude. The _____ attempted to build their lives outside of slavery. Former slaves saw two hopes for their advancement: the ownership of _____ and the procurement of an _____. The _____ attempted to assist African-Americans with this transition, but it was shut down by 1872, part of a general indication of the weariness of the _____ with Reconstruction. Southerners began to _____ their states from black and Republican control through violence and intimidation. With the _____, Reconstruction ended, leaving the South under the control of white _____.

IDENTIFICATION

You should be able to describe the following key terms, concepts, individuals, and places and explain their significance.

Terms and Concepts

Fourteenth Amendment	Fifteenth Amendment
Sharecropping	Ku Klux Klan
Mississippi plan	Redemption
Freedmen's Bureau	Electoral Commission
Black codes	Tenure of Office act
Scalawag	Carpetbagger
Freedpeople	Liberal Republicans
Civil Rights Act of 1875	Civil Rights Act of 1866
Wade-Davis Manifesto	Radical Republicans
Compromise of 1877	

Individuals and Places

Andrew Johnson

Thaddeus Stevens

Rutherford B. Hayes

Edwin Stanton

Susan B. Anthony

Lucy Stone

Memphis riot

Ulysses S. Grant

Benjamin F. Wade

Samuel Tilden

Horace Greeley

New Orleans riot

ESSAY

1. Contrast the Reconstruction programs of Lincoln and Johnson.

2. You are a newly freed slave shortly after the Civil War ends. Explain why four of the following issues were important to you and your friends: marriage, family, names, travel, labor contracts, work done by women and children, schooling, churches, sharecropping.

3. What were the provisions of the Fourteenth Amendment?

4. Why did Republicans in Congress impeach Johnson? Why was he not convicted and removed?

5. Some northerners wished to provide for a distribution of southern lands to former slaves. Describe that plan and the fate it met. Do you think Reconstruction might have had a chance of succeeding *without* some form of land redistribution? Why or why not?

6. Assess the impact of the Reconstruction era. List two major achievements and two major failures of the national program of Reconstruction (presidential and congressional). List two major achievements and two major failures of the radical governments in the South.

CRITICAL THINKING

EVALUATING EVIDENCE (MAPS AND ILLUSTRATIONS)

1. Is the cartoon on page 472 an anti-Grant cartoon? What is the significance of Grant's location? Why is he placed where he is? What is its message about his role in the scandals of his administration?

PRIMARY SOURCE: A Freedman Writes to His Former Master[*]

After the war, Jourdon Anderson, like other former slaves, had to decide for whom he would work and on what terms. In Anderson's case, this decision was especially difficult because his former master wrote and asked him and his family to return to their home in Tennessee. In his response, Anderson, who had fled slavery during the war, voiced his new attitudes in freedom.

Dayton, Ohio, August 7, 1865. To My Old Master, Colonel P. H. Anderson, Big Spring, Tennessee.

SIR: I got your letter and was glad to find that you had not forgotten Jourdon, and that you wanted me to come back and live with you again, promising to do better for me than anybody else can. I have often felt uneasy about you. I thought the Yankees would have hung you long before this for harboring Rebs they found at your house. I suppose they never heard about your going to Col. Martin's to kill the Union soldier that was left by his company in their stable. Although you shot at me twice before I left you, I did not want to hear of your being hurt, and am glad you are still living. It would do me good to go back to the dear old home again and see Miss Mary and Miss Martha and Allen, Esther, Green, and Lee. Give my love to them all, and tell them I hope we will meet in the better world, if not in this. I would have gone back to see you all when I was working in the Nashville Hospital, but one of the neighbors told me Henry intended to shoot me if he ever got a chance.

I want to know particularly what the good chance is you propose to give me. I am doing tolerably well here; I get $25 a month, with victuals and clothing; have a comfortable home for Mandy (the folks here call her Mrs. Anderson), and the children, Milly, Jane and Grundy, go to school and are learning well; the teacher says Grundy has a head for a preacher. They go to Sunday-School, and Mandy and me attend church regularly. We are kindly treated; sometimes we overhear others saying, "Them colored people were slaves" down in Tennessee. The children feel hurt when they hear such remarks, but I tell them it was no disgrace in Tennessee to belong to Col. Anderson. Many darkies would have been proud, as I used to was, to call you master. Now, if you will write and say what wages you will give me, I will be better able to decide whether it would be to my advantage to move back again.

---

[*] From the New York *Tribune*, August 22, 1865. The punctuation has been slightly modified for clarity.

As to my freedom, which you say I can have, there is nothing to be gained on that score, as I got my free-papers in 1864 from the Provost-Marshal-General of the Department at Nashville. Mandy says she would be afraid to go back without some proof that you are sincerely disposed to treat us justly and kindly--and we have concluded to test your sincerity by asking you to send us our wages for the time we served you. This will make us forget and forgive old s[c]ores, and rely on your justice and friendship in the future. I served you faithfully for thirty-two years, and Mandy twenty years. At $25 a month for me, and $2 a week for Mandy, our earnings would amount to $11,680. Add to this the interest for the time our wages has been kept back and deduct what you paid for our clothing and three doctor's visits to me, and pulling a tooth for Mandy, and the balance will show what we are in justice entitled to. Please send the money by Adams Express, in care of V. Winters, esq., Dayton, Ohio. If you fail to pay us for faithful labors in the past we can have little faith in your promises in the future. We trust the good Maker has opened your eyes to the wrongs which you and your fathers have done to me and my fathers, in making us toil for you for generations without recompense. Here I draw my wages every Saturday night, but in Tennessee there was never any pay day for the negroes any more than for the horses and cows. Surely there will be a day of reckoning for those who defraud the laborer of his hire.

In answering this letter please state if there would be any safety for my Milly and Jane, who are now grown up and both good looking girls. You know how it was with poor Malida and Catherine. I would rather stay here and starve and die if it comes to that than have my girls brought to shame by the violence and wickedness of their young masters. You will also please state if there has been any schools opened for the colored children in your neighborhood, the great desire of my life now is to give my children an education, and have them form virtuous habits.

From your old servant,

Jourdan Anderson.

P.S.—Say howdy to George Carter, and thank him for taking the pistol from you when you were shooting at me.

Questions

1. What is Anderson's attitude toward his former master?

2. How has Anderson's life changed in freedom? Do you think he has developed new attitudes as a result?

3. What does freedom mean to Anderson? Does he articulate the meaning of freedom clearly and precisely? Does he think of freedom primarily in terms of its contrast with slavery?

4. Why does Anderson find the idea of returning to the old plantation attractive? Why is he hesitant to do so? Why is he worried about his daughters Milly and Jane?

ANSWER KEY

CHAPTER 1

Multiple Choice	Completion
1. c	overpopulation
2. b	Portugal
3. d	Prester John
4. a	Spain
5. d	Ferdinand and Isabella
6. c	Aztecs
7. a	*encomienda* or *repartimienta*
8. d	religious
9. b	indulgences
10. b	faith
11. c	predestination
12. b	Queen Elizabeth
	Antwerp
	Gilbert
	Sir Walter Raleigh

CHAPTER 2

Multiple Choice	Completion
1. d	Virginia Company of London
2. b	Jamestown
3. a	mortality
4. b	tobacco
5. d	Catholics
6. c	indentured servants
7. d	slavery
8. a	Bacon's Rebellion
9. a	Middle Passage
10. b	sugar
11. c	South Carolina
12. c	James Oglethorpe
	Saint Augustine
	Pueblo Revolt

CHAPTER 3

Multiple Choice

1. c
2. c
3. c
4. c
5. a
6. a
7. d
8. a
9. b
10. d
11. b
12. c

Completion

religious
climate
representative
religion
Anne Hutchinson
heretics
Women
witches
diversity
Iroquois
Quakerism
Dominion of New England
Glorious Revolution
William
Mary

CHAPTER 4

Multiple Choice

1. b
2. c
3. b
4. b
5. b
6. d
7. b
8. a
9. c
10. a
11. c
12. b

Completion

Benjamin Franklin
immigrants
backcountry
Paxton Boys
Regulator
seaports
lowcountry
task system
evangelical Christianity
Jonathan Edwards
George Whitefield
indifference
benign neglect
Englishmen

CHAPTER 5

Multiple Choice	Completion
1. b	English
2. a	Seven Years War
3. c	war
4. c	Proclamation of 1763
5. c	Stamp Act
6. d	representation
7. d	trial by jury
8. a	John Locke
9. b	the Opposition *or* Commonwealthmen
10. a	Townshend Acts
11. d	John Dickinson
12. c	Samuel Adams
	Boston Massacre
	Coercive *or* Intolerable Acts
	First Continental Congress
	Lexington
	Concord

CHAPTER 6

Multiple Choice	Completion
1. d	Battle of Bunker Hill
2. a	Olive Branch Petition
3. a	Declaration of Independence
4. b	George III
5. c	Loyalists
6. d	militias
7. b	New York City
8. d	Philadelphia
9. d	the Battle of Saratoga
10. c	France
11. c	South
	Thomas Sumter
	slaves
	Yorktown

CHAPTER 7

Multiple Choice	**Completion**
1. d	state
2. c	nation
3. d	constitutions
4. a	executive power
5. c	Articles of Confederation
6. c	western
7. b	Northwest Ordinance
8. a	culture
9. b	merit
10. c	Mary Wollstonecraft's
11. c	Benjamin Rush
12. c	Republican motherhood
	Constitution
	James Madison
	Federalist papers
	Self-interest
	virtue
	factions
	Antifederalists
	states

CHAPTER 8

Multiple Choice

1. c
2. a
3. a
4. a
5. a
6. b
7. d
8. a
9. a
10. c
11. b
12. a

Completion

Constitution
coast *or* seaboard
backcountry
agriculture
transportation
barter
water
Benjamin Franklin
Alexander Hamilton
Thomas Jefferson
corruption
aristocracy
Whiskey Rebellion
parties
personal liberty
John Adams
XYZ
Alien and Sedition
Federalist

CHAPTER 9

Multiple Choice

1. d
2. a
3. c
4. b
5. b
6. d
7. a
8. a
9. d
10. d
11. b
12. d

Completion

Washington, D.C.
the Revolution of 1800
impeach
Louisiana
embargo
Lewis and Clark
environment
Black Hoof
Tecumseh
the Prophet
the Second Great Awakening
England
France
neutrality
impressments
War of 1812
Andrew Jackson
Missouri Crisis

CHAPTER 10

Multiple Choice

1. d
2. a
3. b
4. b
5. c
6. b
7. d
8. b
9. d
10. b

Completion

Chauncey Jerome
Market Revolution
domestic
nationalists
cotton gin
steamboat
telegraph
John Marshall
corporation
factory
specialization
interchangeable parts
materialism
middle class
distribution
booms and busts

CHAPTER 11

Multiple Choice

1. a
2. c
3. c
4. c
5. a
6. b
7. a
8. c
9. d
10. a
11. d
12. b

Completion

egalitarian
1824
John Q. Adams
corrupt bargain
common man
Masons
Bank War
common people
Cherokee
Trail of Tears
free blacks
strikebreakers
nullification
federal tariffs
Martin Van Buren
Whig
presidential campaign

CHAPTER 12

Multiple Choice

1. a
2. b
3. d
4. a
5. d
6. c
7. b
8. b
9. a
10. d
11. c
12. d

Completion

stability
religion
revivals
perfectionism
middle class
women
domesticity
transcendentalism
Ralph Waldo Emerson
Utopian
temperance
abolition
William Lloyd Garrison
Seneca Falls

CHAPTER 13

Multiple Choice

1. c
2. c
3. a
4. b
5. d
6. b
7. a
8. a
9. a
10. b
11. d
12. c

Completion

agricultural
slavery
Cotton
single-crop
disease
Upper South
Deep South
yeoman
gang
task
resistance
family
religion
proslavery
1840

CHAPTER 14

Multiple Choice

1. c
2. d
3. b
4. a
5. c
6. c
7. c
8. a
9. d
10. b
11. a
12. d

Completion

manifest destiny
Spain
Mexico
Santa Anna
Mexican
Sam Houston
independent
Overland Trail
Indians
James K. Polk
Great Britain
Zachary Taylor
Mexican War
slavery
Wilmot Proviso
Free Soilers
Henry Clay
1850

CHAPTER 15

Multiple Choice

1. c
2. c
3. b
4. d
5. a
6. d
7. d
8. a
9. c
10. c
11. d
12. b

Completion

Kansas
Lawrence
Pottawatomie Creek
John Brown
sections
railroads
banking and shipping
Stephen Douglas
Missouri Compromise
popular sovereignty
Charles Sumner
Republican
Slave Power
Dred Scott
Harper's Ferry
Abraham Lincoln
1860
secession

CHAPTER 16

Multiple Choice

1. c
2. c
3. a
4. d
5. b
6. c
7. d
8. b
9. b
10. a
11. b
12. a

Completion

South
North
industrial
South
invade
borders
total
civilian
Bull Run *or* Manassas
border states
political
Jefferson Davis
Lincoln
George McClellan
Antietam
Robert E. Lee
war aims
Emancipation Proclamation
Gettysburg
Vicksburg
Ulysses S. Grant
William T. Sherman
March to the Sea
Appamattox
assassinated

CHAPTER 17

Multiple Choice

1. b
2. c
3. d
4. a
5. d
6. b
7. c
8. a
9. d
10. d
11. d
12. b

Completion

reconstructing
generous
Radical
freedmen
Andrew Johnson
veto
black codes
impeachment
Fourteenth and Fifteenth
freedmen
land
education
Freedmen's Bureau
North
redeem
Compromise of 1877
Democrats